Praise for College Appli...

*"Strong essays may not transform modest achievements into winning applications but weak essays can hide what makes your accomplishments distinctive. Umair will **not** let you write a weak essay."*
  - Jeff Brenzel, former Dean of Undergraduate Admissions, Yale

"A wildly engaging, honest, and irreverent book. You will die to share its insights with friends and family. Khan puts the focus on what moves and drives a young person to act in the world. This book offers a concrete action plan for college essay writing, and frankly, for life. We should all read it."
  - Dr. Clare Talwalker, Faculty, U.C. Berkeley

"A warm, easy-to-read, and practical guide to a most important part of college application, the personal essay. As a professor with over 20 years' experience in the student selection process, I can't emphasize enough the importance of clear, concise, interesting college essays. Khan's book is a "must-read" for anyone applying to college."
  - Dr. Charles Browne, Professor of Applied Linguistics Meiji Gakuin University, Japan

*"This essential guide to the application essay writing process can change your essay from **weakest link** to **deciding factor** in your favour!"*
  - Thomas Hayton, Former Director, Macmillan Education; former Application Coach, The Princeton Review and Kaplan

"Fun AND instructive! Applicants will find the before and after versions of real college essays especially helpful."
  - Radhika Nagpal, Professor, Harvard University

"Khan's entertaining and informative look at college admissions provides a plan to win the college application game and also imparts wider wisdom on how to play the game of life."
  - Paul Riley, former Director ELT, Oxford University Press

"As a college professor for 20+ years, I have read many essays (mostly for graduate school). All I can say is, I hope my sons read this book and heed the advice as they write their essays. Mr. Khan, any advice on grant writing?"
  - Dr. Irfan Essa, Associate Dean & Professor, College of Computing, GeorgiaTech

"Congratulations to Umair Khan on the publication of **College Application Hacked**! The advice on writing style is pithy and equally applicable to other forms of high-risk correspondence."
   - **Joseph Noble, Head of Partnerships and Innovation, Oxford University Press**

"A practical, informative, easily accessible, and often amusing guide to the process of writing a successful college essay. Writing that essay still won't be a cinch... but it just got a whole lot easier."
   - **Munis Faruqui, Associate Professor, U.C. Berkeley**

"The college essay may be the most important essay most of us ever write. Before you write a single word, read this book. Umair lays out the keys to rocking this part of your application."
   - **Charles Huang, Trustee, U.C. Berkeley Foundation; Co-creator, Guitar Hero**

"The criteria identified by Umair are EXACTLY what college admission staff have in mind when reading application essays!"
   - **Mustafa Menai, Faculty, University of Pennsylvania**

"An easy read that helps kids and parents cut through the confusing advice from college counselors and understand what makes an essay stand out. Even though it's primarily targeted at undergrads, I will recommend it to anyone approaching me for business school advice."
   - **Imran Sayeed, Sr. Lecturer, MIT Sloan**

"An insightful book for college applicants (and their parents), with lessons on how to write fun-to-read essays that stand out."
   - **Khurram Afridi, Assistant Professor, University of Colorado**

"A great guide to clear and effective writing – even beyond the college essay – that could be of benefit to everyone."
   - **Raka Ray, Professor, U. C. Berkeley**

"I hate Umair. Why couldn't he have written this amazingly practical and no BS book when I was applying to colleges? Umair expertly breaks the process down into such easy-to-understand pieces, it's like he's plugged into every college admission office. I actually feel sorry for the students that don't read this book."
   - **Joe Miller, GM & Vice President, Cengage Learning**

COLLEGE APPLICATION HACKED

1. The College Essay

How to write a killer personal statement in which no pet dies

Umair Khan

"College Application Hacked: 1. The College Essay" by Umair Khan

© 2017 Umair Khan

All rights reserved. No portion of this book may be reproduced or distributed in any form without permission from the author.

For permissions, feedback, and other enquiries, contact: ukhan@alum.mit.edu

To learn more about the book and its sequel, *College Application Hacked - Part 2: Crafting a Winning College Application* visit: www.collegeapplicationhacked.com

Original cover design: Heri Susanto & Dian Abidin ("Omake")

Illustrations and Graphic Art: Borislav Ivanov

Featured on the back cover: Pi, the author's golden doodle dog

Imprint: Burns Road Press
First Printing: August 2017

ISBN: 978-0-9989278-0-0 (e-book)
ISBN: 978-0-9989278-1-7 (print)

First Edition

To
all the poor that were helped,
the sick that were healed,
the clubs that never were,
and the pets that died
in college application essays.

Also to
Amara, Sahlik, and Samar

Contents

1. Prologue: Who, How, Why 8
2. The Three Things Colleges Really Want 12
3. The Only Thing That Matters 15
4. A Seven-Step Program 18
5. Step 1: Study the Prompts 20
6. Step 2: The Facts of Your Life 23
7. Step 3: So What's Your Story? 26
8. Step 4: A Horrible First Draft 30
9. Step 5: Another First Draft 33
10. Step 6: The Hook(s) 35
11. Step 7: Revision and the Seven Stylistic Sins 42
12. What Got Me into MIT 47
13. Essay: The Activist Who Spoke Too Much 51
14. Essay: The Dentist Who Hated Bugs Bunny 57
15. Essay: The Student and the Social Contract 64
16. Essay: The Economist Who Forgot Word Economy 69
17. Essay: The Animal Lover with Attention Deficit 75
18. Essay: The Day Creativity Died 80
19. Essay: The Student Who Forgot the Prompt 83
20. Essay: The Bookworm Who Ate SAT Word Lists 90
21. Essay: The Boy Who Ignored Word Limits 94
22. Essay: We are All Chocolates 98
23. Essay: The Romantic Aeronautical Engineer 101

24. Essay: Warning – Turbulence Ahead 104
25. 'Why Our College' & Other Supplemental Essays 106
26. A Word on Cheating: Don't 111
27. Theorem: Applying to College is Stress-free 114
28. The Greatest Finish Ever 118
Acknowledgments 120
Preview: College Application Hacked – Part 2 121
About the Author 122
Index 123

1. Prologue: Who, How, Why

Who should read this book?
Over 3 million students will apply to colleges alongside you. The Ivy League Schools alone will review nearly 200,000 applications. Your essay will get 3 minutes[1].

This book will show you how to write a much better essay than you can today. You should read this book if you are:

- A high school junior or senior applying soon to colleges.
- A college junior or senior applying to grad school
- A student applying for scholarships and fellowships
- Someone wishing to write un-cringeworthy prose

Who wrote this book?
I applied to and was accepted at Princeton, MIT (twice), Stanford (twice), Yale, Cornell, Dartmouth, Brown, and Carnegie Mellon (I chose MIT for both undergraduate and graduate studies). Yes, I had good grades but so did many,

---

[1] Average time an admissions officer spends on a personal statement.

many others who did not get into these colleges. The difference was how I presented *my story* in my essays.

Now an Education Technology entrepreneur in Silicon Valley, California, I regularly coach high school students on how to tell *their stories* in an authentic and compelling way.

I wrote this book for you, to help you tell your story.

How is this book different?
This book does not:

- include interviews with admissions officers asking you to be yourself.
- have a collection of perfect essays that won the Ivy League lottery. (You can get those online for free. Besides, such essays teach you as much about perfecting your essay as staring at a Rembrandt teaches you to paint.)

This book does:

- tell you step-by-step how to construct your story and write and refine your personal statement.
- pick apart **real essays** to show you exact do's and don'ts. Among the many samples, you will find instances similar to your own style. Reading their critiques will be like having your writing analyzed and improved by a college coach.
- show you several before-and-after's, NOT just the after's. It takes you from raw first drafts (good ones and bad ones), through analysis of the writings, to final, polished essays. You get to learn from other people's mistakes – less painful than learning from yours.

Why should you read this book?
This book will help you:

- learn a **seven step program** to organize and construct your personal statements.
- see how you should create your story arc.
- encounter the **seven deadly stylistic sins** to avoid.
- review real college essays going from first drafts to final, polished statements.
- learn the **three things colleges really want.**
- find out what is the **only thing that matters.**

This book will also get rid of your biggest college application fears:

1. You must be a great writer to write a great college essay.
2. Without exceptional grades you are doomed.
3. You need a well-rounded extracurricular resume to even be considered at good colleges.

Most importantly, this book will ensure your college essays do not have passages such as these:

"The art of manipulating manual dexterity with complex knowledge of science and technology can literally transform patient quality and outlook of life. It makes the profession unlike any other service and has made me religiously committed to becoming a superior dental surgeon. My desire to actualize my abilities for the betterment of society is a decisive factor in my career choice."

"I cannot articulate the extent of effect that my experience with the Congressman's office has had on me. I had the opportunity to

learn and apply most crucial skills in leadership, diligence, and situation control."

"The challenges that my history teacher provided to me two years ago continues to drive me to accomplish new feats, and pushes my limits further each and everyday. I would indefinitely make the same decisions over again if faced with this situation and others."

"Love. Love is what matters to me…. Love is not only something you can give, show or receive, it is something you can want as well. Love brings with itself a potpourri of emotions and feelings. Desire, will, and passion are just some of the package's constituents. Science tells us that the universe is constantly in flux; it's what allows our friendships and our love to constantly shape us."

2. The Three Things Colleges Really Want

If you type "what are colleges looking for in applicants?" into Google Search, you will see two types of responses from admissions experts:

- Your academic resume should have: High GPA, rigorous coursework, strong SAT/ACT scores, college readiness, extracurricular activities, work experience, great recommendations. Exceptional academic projects/awards would be nice.
- Your personal qualities should include: leadership, initiative, maturity, integrity, a sense of social responsibility, a commitment to service, passion for a non-academic interest, special talents. Strong writing skills would be nice too.

Blindingly obvious. Not very helpful.

Colleges are looking for THREE things in an applicant:

1. Will this kid be a SUCCESS (i.e., rich & famous)?
2. Will this kid make other students HAPPY?
3. Will this kid add a DISTINCTIVE talent to our mix?

1. Will this kid be a SUCCESS?
Colleges want their graduates to be highly successful in fortune and fame creation and give a good bit back. This

means your essay has to say (in an un-clichéd way): *"I have the self-motivation and work ethics to succeed"*.

Now, you may not make a lot of money but if you become a Nobel prize winning biologist or economic advisor to the president, that will do just as well. Colleges love to shine in their alumni's fame. So your essay has to say (in a cool way): *"When I commit to {X}, I don't stop until I become the best at {X}"*.

2. Will this kid make other students HAPPY?

Colleges want you to make other students happy so that these students are more willing to share their success with their alma mater. Basically they want you to be social, helpful, and memorable, not a sarcastic, arrogant jerk. Your essay must show (in an unboring way): *"I am interesting, friendly, and well-loved for my humility and humor"*.

3. Will this kid add a DISTINCTIVE talent to our mix?

Great colleges are not simply rank-ordering applicants and picking the top percentile (or three). Admissions officers have to stock up science labs, populate orchestras, fill track & field rosters, recruit humanities majors, etc. Each year they try to piece together an exceptional puzzle with students with distinctive interests and diverse backgrounds. They want you to be a special piece that fills a gap. So your essay must point out (in a distinctive voice): *"I have a unique talent or background to add to your mix"*.

So where do grades fit in? Does work experience really matter? How about sports and clubs? And SATs and ACTs? Demonstrated leadership skills? All of these are pointers to future success. Colleges look at grades, work experience, athletic achievements, SAT scores, etc., **as indicators of you (a) fitting nicely into college and (b)** *succeeding enormously out of it.* (Which is why if Dad is a billionaire or an ex-president, you may get in despite the *meh* GPA and minimal self-motivation.)

When colleges read your essay they are asking: "after graduating, will this applicant create success (i.e., wealth and fame) to give back? And while in college, will this person help others enjoy their college experience?"

When you write your essay, make sure you ask yourself the same questions.

3. The Only Thing That Matters

Self-motivated (adj.): Motivated to do or achieve something because of one's own enthusiasm or interest, without needing pressure from others."
- Oxford English Dictionary

Great colleges are looking for the potential for success. More precisely, they are looking for the **self-motivation** that leads to success.

Do you need parents or teachers or friends to get the best out of you? Do you need deadlines and dread to stay motivated? Do you get excited about something but give it up when the grind starts? Do you have a compelling talent or passion that you have done very little about? If so, you are not self motivated.

If you *are not* self-motivated, you are likely not going to get into a great college.

If you *are* self-motivated, you don't need a great college (but are likely to get into one anyway).

This is the college application paradox.

The 9 Year-old Who Wrote to the President

What does self-motivation look like? Here is the story of a self-motivated girl and her road to Harvard.

In 1957, a girl wrote to the president of the USA in protest of segregation. She lived in a state (Virginia) that was strongly for segregating blacks and whites. She wrote the letter without her parents or teachers telling her to do so or helping her (or even knowing about it). Here is what she wrote:

DEAR MR. EISENHOWER,

     I AM NINE YEARS OLD AND I AM WHITE BUT I HAVE MANY FEELINGS ABOUT SEGREGATION. WHY SHOULD PEOPLE FEEL THAT WAY BECAUSE THE COLOR OF THE SKIN? IF I PAINTED MY FACE BLACK I WOULDN'T BE LET IN ANY PUBLIC SCHOOLS etc. MY FEELINGS HAVEN'T CHANGED, JUST THE COLOR OF MY SKIN.

     LONG AGO ON CHRISTMAS DAY JESUS CHRIST WAS BORN. AS YOU REMEMBER HE WAS BORN TO SAVE THE WORLD. NOT ONLY WHITE PEOPLE BUT BLACK YELLOW RED AND BROwn.

     COLORED PEOPLE AREN'T GIVEN A CHANCE. "THEY DONT HAVE A GOOD EDUCATION," SaYS MANY PEOPLE. Is It their fault if THEIR FATHERS ARE SO POOR THEY Must be taken out at an early age TO FIND JOBS? ONLY ABOUT 2% of our prep SCHOOLS are for colored people.

     SO WHAT IF THEIR SKIN IS BLACK? THEY STILL HAVE FEELINGS BUT MOST OF ALL ARE GOD'S PEOPLE!

PLEASE MR EISENHOWER, PLEASE TRY AND HAVE SCHOOLS and other THiNGS accEPT COLORED PEOPLE.

Sincerly, [sic]

CATHERINE DREW GILPiN

The girl who wrote this letter was admitted to some great colleges. She studied at Bryn Mawr and the University of Pennsylvania. And while she did not study at Harvard, she did, in 2011, become the first woman to be appointed President of Harvard University.

4. A Seven-Step Program

In applying to colleges, as in much else in life, you should:

1. **Start early**: Allow plenty of time to cure your essay of its ills and sins.
2. **Get organized**: Give yourself time to be creative by being organized.
3. **Take small steps**: Build momentum by planning and achieving milestones.

The seven-step program below will help you with nos. 2 and 3; no. 1 is up to you:

1. Study the prompts.
2. Collect the facts of your life.
3. Create your "story arc".
4. Write that crappy first draft.
5. Write another first draft.
6. Nail "The Hook(s)".
7. Revise – and avoid the seven stylistic sins.

Ideally you should start this program the summer between your junior and senior years. This is because (a) you will be doing plenty of other things, (b) these steps can't be rushed, and (c) you are not writing one but four to eight essays (when you include supplemental statements) and you will not be able to write them *all* in parallel (this is not a dare, just reality).

If you are reading this with just 8 weeks left, you should plan to give a week to each step and do it as an 8-week program. If you are reading this with 8 days left, read quickly.

5. Step 1: Study the Prompts

"Begin at the beginning," the King said, very gravely,
"and go on till you come to the end: then stop."
- Lewis Carroll, Alice in Wonderland

Start by registering for the Common App and read the essay prompts. Some of your top choice colleges may not be on the Common App or may have supplementary essay topics: read these prompts as well.

The Common Application Prompts
Here are the current personal statement prompts for the Common App:

1. Some students have a background, identity, interest, or talent that is so meaningful they believe their application would be incomplete without it. If this sounds like you, then please share your story.
2. The lessons we take from failure can be fundamental to later success. Recount an incident or time when you experienced failure. How did it affect you, and what did you learn from the experience?
3. Reflect on a time when you challenged a belief or idea. What prompted you to act? Would you make the same decision again?

4. Describe a problem you've solved or a problem you'd like to solve. It can be an intellectual challenge, a research query, an ethical dilemma- anything that is of personal importance, no matter the scale. Explain its significance to you and what steps you took or could be taken to identify a solution.
5. Discuss an accomplishment or event, formal or informal, that marked your transition from childhood to adulthood within your culture, community, or family.

The UC Application Prompts

Here are the 8 current prompts for the University of California Application (350 words maximum per for response – you choose any four):

1. Describe an example of your leadership experience in which you have positively influenced others, helped resolve disputes, or contributed to group efforts over time.
2. Every person has a creative side, and it can be expressed in many ways: problem solving, original and innovative thinking, and artistically, to name a few. Describe how you express your creative side.
3. What would you say is your greatest talent or skill? How have you developed and demonstrated that talent over time?
4. Describe how you have taken advantage of a significant educational opportunity or worked to overcome an educational barrier you have faced.
5. Describe the most significant challenge you have faced and the steps you have taken to overcome this

challenge. How has this challenge affected your academic achievement?
6. Describe your favorite academic subject and explain how it has influenced you.
7. What have you done to make your school or your community a better place?
8. What is the one thing that you think sets you apart from other candidates applying to the University of California?

Assignment #1

Here is your first assignment: mull these prompts for a few days. Which ones excite your interest? Write down why they move you. Can you think of events or episodes that fit well with some of these prompts? Write these down as well.

6. Step 2: The Facts of Your Life

In this step you will collect the facts of your life in **five lists**. Start by jotting down short points – no need to elaborate just yet.

List 1: Interests
- List your interests out in these two categories:
    - Academic/Intellectual (subjects, career choices)
    - non-academic (sports, hobbies, etc.), strong likes/dislikes
- Mark your *top* passion(s) or interest(s).

List 2: Achievements
- Awards, distinctions, recognitions, actions you are proud of: write them all down. Nothing is too trivial (go ahead, include the Vice Presidency of the Harry Potter Fan Club).

List 3: Events and Experiences
- What were some significant events in your past? They can be significant events – when you won the science fair or state championship – or memorable experiences – an unforgettable trip to South America or your first day as student body president.
- Include all work and volunteer experience. And don't forget The Crazy Stuff – like when you tried to

set the world record for most hours spent in a swimming pool.

List 4: Qualities and Talents
- What are your unique qualities and traits?
- Don't confuse talent with interests. Your interests may be related to your unique qualities, they may give insights into your talents, but they are not the same. For example:
    - Interest = Love of Chess ; Talent = Good at strategic thinking
    - Achievement = President of Debate Club; Talent = Great at oral communication

List 5: People
- Influencers: folks you may be compelled to write about or mention in your essays.
- Brainstormers: people you will discuss your ideas with.
- Reviewers: folks who are good at writing.

Next, expand each list by adding details. Write down punch lines, humorous bits and pieces, how you felt then, how you feel now looking back, etc. These don't need to be polished nuggets, but they need to be nuggets. Save these up for use in your essays.

Finally, highlight the events, achievements, and experiences that show *self-motivation*. These will anchor your essay.

Events List: Bird Traps and Broken Wings
Here is the events list of someone applying as an Animal Science major who wants to show an enduring and self-motivated passion for animal care:

1. Made a bird trap when I was 8 with my dad's help
2. Nursed a baby dove whose wing was broken and taught it how to fly
3. Started lizard catching service
4. Almost set Guinness world record for staying in pool longest

Here are expansions of the first two items in the list:

- *My dad told me that he had tried making a bird trap with a box, stick, string, and bird food but that he was never able to catch anything. I took this as a challenge and decided to make one of those traps. I was so determined to catch a bird and promised myself I wouldn't give up until I did. I waited in my backyard with the trap for two days until I was finally able to catch a bird.*
- *My neighbor brought me a baby dove with cuts all over one of its wings. He asked if I could take care of it, because he knew that I loved helping animals. I had never had to care for an injured baby bird before, so I wasn't really sure what to do. I looked up online of how to clean the birds' wounds, what to feed it. It took many days for the wound on his wing to heal, and after that I still had to teach him to fly.*

These lists should help you not just with your essays but with other parts of the application as well.

7. Step 3: So What's Your Story?

Think of your favorite book or movie. It probably has:

- ONE main plot (and maybe a subplot), not five or six storylines
- A few characters that hook you, not an ensemble cast with bit parts
- A seamless build up to a climactic scene, not sudden, unbelievable jumps in action

Your essay – *and the rest of your application* – must read like an engaging and believable story. No one wants to read a disjointed laundry list of events and actions. The picture of you in your essay must be clean, clear, and appealing.

Your Story Arc
Take the lists you made in Step 2 and distill what's special about you down to two, maybe three, things. It is important to be deep and narrow, not shallow and wide. Pick the incident(s) or achievement(s) that shows extraordinary self-motivation.

Now write your story arc - *a summary of your life story and you as a person* - in a paragraph (or two). Think of it as the plot summary of a movie (in this case, of your life). This paragraph is going to be the story arc in your essays and in your college app.

As you write your story, make sure:

- Your arc starts early [or at least not in the last one year]: There is nothing worse than a murder mystery in which the author introduces a miracle solution in the last chapter. Please don't thrust upon the admissions officer a lifelong dedication to human health as shown by the internship you did last month. If you have an abiding interest or talent, there should be plenty of evidence (i.e., events and achievements) over many years.
- Your arc stays till today [or at least till the last year]: No one will believe the overriding passion for photography you have had since you were 6, if you have done NOTHING about it these past four years.
- Your arc is unbroken during the intervening years [or at least the breaks are not multi-year gaps]
- Your interests, extracurricular activities, work experience support your arc as much as your essays. You cannot write an essay about your love of Music or Math or Literature and not have your work, academics, and extracurricular activities back this up.

Story Arc Examples

Here are some story arcs I have seen over the years in college applications (note the strong focus on one interest or talent):

"I love chess. I was a state chess champion in elementary school. I taught chess to younger kids when I entered high school (I still teach chess). I also love Math. I love solving problems and I want to see what I get on the Putnam my freshman year. The two men I admire the most are Alan Turing and Bobby Fischer. I want to

take a lot of Math courses at College but I am not sure what my major will be."

"I am an ardent booklover and a writer. I love the smell of old books and visiting bookstores. I got the booklover gene from my dad who has a huge book collection at home. I won an essay competition in 8th grade and got a free trip to Washington, DC. I am gathering 12 of my short stories into a collection that I want to self-publish on Amazon. I also love the performing arts and have been in several plays at school and at local community centers. Besides literature and writing, I want to explore theater and film in college. I hope to write an award-winning Broadway play before I turn 30."

"By 4th grade I had read EVERY animal story in my elementary school library. I have owned over 11 pet rabbits, hens, mice, and dogs. I have interned at an animal hospital every summer during high school (I even got to assist in surgery). I started a pet-sitting service in our neighborhood and a "lizard removal" service. I also love to write. I want to study animal science and be a vet (I think). I also want to be a famous writer like James Herriot (All Creatures Great and Small)."

"I love to code. I started coding in 5th grade. I got into Artificial Intelligence (AI) when I was in 9th grade. I read Marvin Minsky's, The Society of Mind, in 10th grade. I have seen "2001: A Space Odyssey 11 times". I did an internship in Natural Language Processing (NLP) and speech recognition with a company in Germany the summer after 11th grade. I want to do research in Brain and Cognitive Science."

Be Authentic
Try not to write someone else's story, someone whom you think the colleges would love. You are probably not a great fiction writer and the admissions officer has read thousands of such fictions.

You have enough to work with. Focus on shaping it into a story that shows why you are the prize catch.

Wishing for a Better Hand

At this point in your application process, you will find yourself wishing you had more to work with:

> "I wish I had done more freshman year."
> "I wish I had started my essays earlier."
> "I wish I had gotten a better GPA. "
> "I wish I had more work experience."
> "I wish I had more time."

At such moments remind yourself of the exchange between Frodo and the wizard, Gandalf, in The Lord of the Rings. Frodo has had a rough few months, with more misery to come. As a Hobbit, he is not the ideal candidate for the mission. And so he says to Gandalf:

"I wish the ring had never come to me. I wish none of this had ever happened."

And Gandalf replies: "So do all who live to see such times. But that is not for you to decide. All you have to decide is what to do with the time that is given to you." [2]

A good thought to remember when applying to colleges. And at all other times.

---

[2] From the movie, The Lord of the Rings: The Fellowship of the Ring (Newline 2001).

8. Step 4: A Horrible First Draft

Perfect is the enemy of good.
- Italian Proverb

If you try to come up with a dream opening, that perfect ending, crisp sentences, and memorable metaphors your first time around, you will be nursing a writer's block until December.

You have made your lists, written your story arc, and chosen your first prompt. Here is what you must do now:

1. Treat your essay just like a school assignment that's due **very soon:**
    - Set a deadline no more than a few days out.
    - Set aside time every day to write.
2. Start by making an outline
    - Write a list of key points you want to make for this prompt (just like you always do for a school essay).
    - Pick a focus from your lists of events, achievements, interests, people, and qualities. It should be something that (a) you truly want to write about and (b) best highlights your self-motivation.
    - Avoid making the following your focus:
        o Personal tragedy (death, divorce, etc.): these are weighty themes that most people cannot

do justice to, especially while highlighting themselves.
- Sports event: winning that match may have been exhilarating, but will it make for an exhilarating essay?
- Generic volunteer work or extracurricular activity: hard to rise above the crowd if you pick a topic most often picked by the crowd.

3. **JUST WRITE**
    - Don't worry about a cool beginning or ending.
    - Don't worry about The Hook (we will deal with that shortly).
    - Don't worry about the word limit.
    - Don't start thinking about three essays in parallel: focus on one prompt.
    - Just concentrate on completing your first draft with a beginning, a main plot, an end, and a hero (you).

Great Expectations? Not Yet
As you can tell by the title of this chapter, no one is expecting Hamlet or Harry Potter. As you can tell by the titles of the next two chapters, you will do a rewrite (and you can't do a rewrite without doing a write). Finally, as you can tell by the titles of most of the remaining chapters, this book is full of hair-raising first drafts all of which led to impressive final versions. Here is one such first draft.

Prompt: *Every person has a creative side, and it can be expressed in many ways…Describe how you express your creative side.*

I express my creative side by creating. From the young age of 6, my passion about Legos had me putting hours into creating complex structures *from the thousands of bricks scattered around my floor.* Although I outgrew my joy of stacking bricks I found a new one in chess. Playing against thousands of people both online and tournaments each game I found a new way of checkmating them. My innovative gameplay helped me win first place in the Cal-State Chess Championship and the Age Level Tournament and a rating of 1500. I then started teaching chess to beginning and intermediate players. Creating a website called, chesstutoring.com, I taught both chess and math at my local library to kids ages 4-12. Each class I would make a multitude of chess puzzles and tactics for my students to fiddle with.

As the President of our chess club, in 2014, every Monday lunch I would think of fun ways to keep our members entertained; for example we had many games like "Bug house" and chess tower competitions. My unique thinking style also came in handy in 8th grade; after a couple courses in java I began using my creativity to make levels and games. After receiving a internship from a company called, in the summer of my junior year, I used the right side of my brain to design over a hundred levels for their game called, "DoggyRun." My work on DoggyRun helped me receive another internship with the company. This summer I helped design over 50 quizzes for their latest app called, "bookquiz". My contribution to both apps led to me being recognized in the credits.

9. Step 5: Another First Draft

"Those who cannot learn from history are condemned to repeat it."
– George Santanya

Before you do a rewrite, you must learn what is wrong with your first draft. The best way to learn is to ask.

The Ask
Look at your first draft and ask yourself these nine questions:

1. Did I choose the prompt because it sounded cool (but don't really care for it)?
2. Is my opening boring? (How about the middle? And the ending?) [Hint: read the next chapter]
3. Am I being too gimmicky or wacky?
4. Have I answered the question(s) asked?
5. Am I exaggerating the importance to me of an event, experience, or interest? *[No? Really? Are you sure there is no melodrama? Really?]*
6. Am I trying to say too much (and leaving the reader confused)?
7. Did I forget whom I am writing ABOUT?
8. Did I forget whom I am writing FOR?
9. Is my essay disconnected from my application?

Remember List 5 in Step 2 (The Facts of Your Life)? Now is the time to call on people you know who read more and write better than you. Ask them the questions above (at least the first six).

Use these questions to pick out the gems – ideas, sentences, phrases – from the carcass of your first draft. Use them in the outline of the rewrite. Also pick out what does not work: guard against these creeping back in

In rewriting your essay, ***don't copy and paste***. Open a new file. This is another first draft, not a revision of your first draft.

As you start on your final first draft, it is time to come up with The Hook(s).

10. Step 6: The Hook(s)

The Hook is usually defined as the opening sentences that "hook in" the reader and gets them to read on. For your college essay, you will need **three** hooks:

- The Opening Hook: A beginning that intrigues and draws in the reader
- The Theme Hook: A theme or construct that makes your essay stand out
- The Ending Hook: The parting thought that lingers

If this sounds like your whole essay has to hook in your reader, you are right.

The Opening Hook
By way of limbering up, here are some great openings lines from fiction:

"One morning, when Gregor Samsa woke from troubled dreams, he found himself transformed in his bed into a gigantic insect." [Franz Kafka]

"It was the best of times, it was the worst of times" [Charles Dickens]

"It was the day grandmother exploded." [Iain M. Banks]

"Many years later, as he faced the firing squad, Colonel Aureliano Buendía was to remember that distant afternoon when his father took him to discover ice." [Gabriel Garcia Marquez]

More to the task at hand, here are some intriguing openings from successful college essays:

"I change my name each time I place an order at Starbucks." (Admitted to Stanford)

"Some fathers might disapprove of their children handling noxious chemicals in the garage." (Admitted to Stanford)

"I recite ancient Chinese poems, but adore Jane Austen. I devour spicy chicken feet, but drool for ballpark franks. I dream in Chinese, but think in English." (Admitted to MIT)

"When I was in eighth grade I couldn't read." (Admitted to Stanford)

Opening Hook Examples

Here is a unique way of opening a "describe the world you come from" essay:

For 18 years my natural habitat has been Carnelle Court, the cul-de-sac where I grew up. Think United Nations meets the San Diego Zoo. Ethnicities: Bulgarian, Israeli, German, Peruvian, Chinese, Indian, Pakistani, Midwestern-American, Russian. Pets: butterflies, fish, chickens, dogs, bunnies, lizards, cats, birds, hamsters.

Here are before and after versions of an opening paragraph in a "how do you express your creative side?" essay:

BEFORE:

I express my creative side by creating. From the young age of 6, my passion about Legos had me putting hours into creating complex structures from the thousands of bricks scattered around my floor. Although I outgrew my joy of stacking bricks I found a new one in chess.

AFTER:
I was a California State Junior Chess Champion at 8, started a chess tutoring business at 13, helped design one of the most popular puzzle games on the App store at 15, and was ranked in the top 40 (out of 10 million players) in Hearthstone, at 17.

Memorable beginnings are more art than science, but here, nevertheless, are some tips:

- Don't be melodramatic. Memorable prose is effortless.
- Don't be cute for cuteness' sake. It comes across as immature and desperate, and you don't want that to be the first impression.
- Don't dig yourself into a hole you can't come out of. A cool, quirky opening is useless if it does not flow naturally into the essay body.
- Start with a dialogue, perhaps.
- Describe an unusual scene or person with minute attention to detail.
- As always, avoid clichés.
- A bit of humor never hurts (just don't overdo it).
- Careful with famous quotes. Starting with a quotation is like using a stock photo. If you must start with a quote, follow it with an unexpected sentiment or observation.
- Ask yourself if you find your opening compelling. If your answer is no, scrap it. If your answer is yes, ask others.

The Theme Hook
The Theme Hook is a compelling construct that binds your essay. It makes your essay memorable while allowing you to tell your story.

The best theme hooks let you tie together a vivid opening, the main body, and a memorable ending. Theme hooks can be unboring: your love of nature expressed in a series of hiking disaster anecdotes; a memorable encounter in travels abroad, what you learnt from your pets. Or they can be outright zany: how all your important life lessons can be traced back to grocery shopping with mom; an imaginary conversation with your favorite dead poet; why you want to time travel back to your 5th birthday. You can get quirky theme hooks from some college essay prompts themselves:

- U. of Chicago: What is square one, and can you actually go back to it?
- U. of Chicago: What's odd about odd numbers?
- Tufts: What does #YOLO mean to you?
- Yale: You have been granted a free weekend next month. How will you spend it?"

Never choose a theme - no matter how clever - that does not let you fully tell your story. If the theme hampers your storytelling, chuck it.

Theme Hook Example: Champion Egg Layer
Here is an excerpt from an essay (in the University of California application) where the applicant talks about her greatest quality (empathy) - as asked by the essay prompt - by using a pet chicken named Akaky Akakievich as the theme hook. This leads to rather nice opening and ending hooks, and a pleasing cohesive theme.

Opening:
   I have a pet chicken named Akaky Akakievich. A soft-spoken Rhode Island Red, Akaky's crowning achievement in life came when she laid two eggs, one a double-yolker. Champion egg-laying aside, Akaky is special because she embodies the gift given to me by my love of animals: their enduring gift to me is empathy.

Body:
I have always loved animals. I have always loved books. Which passion arose first is my own chicken-and-egg riddle.
   [....]
   My empathy powers my activism and makes my politics lean left of insincerity. Which is where Akaky the hen comes in.
   [....]
   The day after I finished the Omnivore's Dilemma, I wrote an expose' in my school newspaper on factory farming, corporate inhumanity, and consumer apathy. The week after, I bought my first chicken, Akaky. A month later our neighbors had backyard chickens too

Ending:
   I don't know exactly what profession my activism will choose. I do know that a life filled with empathy has little room for apathy. And for that I am grateful to literature, to animals, and to Akaky Akakiavich.

The Ending Hook
Here are a few things to remember as you prepare to leave the admission officer with a memorable ending:

- Don't end with a whimper: Leave with a powerful thought or idea.
- Don't try *too* hard to end with a bang either *[I know, I know]*.

- Short sentences have power. End with a short sentence.
- Avoid summarizing. A laundry list of qualities is not a memorable ending.
- End with a dialogue, perhaps?
- See if you can echo the beginning.

Ending Hook Examples
Here are the Before and After versions of the ending of an essay requesting financial aid consideration (note the power of short sentences in the After).

BEFORE:
Therefore, I request LSE to offer me a scholarship. In return I will give my scholastic and personal best to LSE and avail every opportunity to befriend, enrich and help shape its diverse student community.

AFTER
All my ambitions are "such stuff as dreams are made on". The first step is an LSE education. You hold the financial key. And I await your decision.

Here is an ending where a book-lover talks about how her parents inspired her love of reading. Note how the verbose language in Before makes it less memorable.

BEFORE:
My parents instilled within me the invaluable traits of imagination, versatility, creativity, and perseverance, to name a precious few. What my parents have done for me is nothing short of ineffable.

AFTER
To ask what I can in turn do for my parents is a bit like asking, as the philosopher did: "How can a blade of grass repay the

warmth of the summer sun?" Reading and writing forever would be a good start.

The Last Word
Memorable writing hooks you in – beginning, middle, *and* end. The sentences that follow could be cool beginnings, thoughts that grab you in the middle, or memorable endings:

In the multiple choice of my childhood, my parents always supported me when I stubbornly chose None of the Above; also when I chose All of the Above.

It took 27 rounds of coffee to find my voice, but it was worth the wait.

[Life] is a tale told by an idiot, full of sound and fury, signifying nothing.[3]

Be memorable.

---

[3] With apologies to Shakespeare, who, I am sure, would have written a killer personal statement.

11. Step 7: Revision and the Seven Stylistic Sins

"If I had had more time, I would have written a shorter letter."
– Mark Twain

So far we have discussed substance. In this chapter we will talk about style. There are seven stylistic sins nearly all college applicants are guilty of. Review and revise your essay to make sure it is NOT:

1. Wordy and long-winded
2. Boring
3. Clogged with big words
4. Cliché ridden
5. Sensationalist
6. Tone deaf
7. Riddled with careless mistakes

1. Be brief

Mark Twain once wrote at the end of long letter: "If I had had more time, I would have written a shorter letter". Being concise, writing crisp sentences, is hard, grinding work. It takes endless reviews and ruthless cuts. Ask yourself: how impactful is EACH sentence? Each paragraph? Proofreaders help: neutral eyes are better at spotting unneeded details.

Won't the word count restriction force me to be brief, you ask? Not necessarily. You can be pithy in a 1000-word essay or long winded in writing a 100-word paragraph. It is the "signal to noise ratio" that matters.

Never say something in two paragraphs that could be said in one sentence. Perhaps the last two paragraphs illustrate this point well. The following before and after versions of a college essay's opening illustrate it even better:

ORIGINAL: In economics, theoretically the market system is the best allocating mechanism but practically it causes market failure similarly one might find the content of a course suitable for him but without any work experience one cannot decide if he has the motivation and the mindset to study a course. Working at DuPont I got an opportunity to observe many occupations, keeping in mind my skill set and passion for finance, a career in accountancy was the best fit for me. [80 words]

REVISED: Finance has always topped my scholastic interests but what really sparked my attraction to Accounting was an internship at DuPont. [20 words]

Remember, a bore is someone who leaves nothing unsaid (Oscar Wilde). Which brings us to our second sin.

2. Don't be boring

You have chosen your theme and substance to be unboring (hopefully). Now guard against your writing boring the heck out of the admissions officer.

Ask yourself: Do you as a reader find it interesting? What about others you show it to. Ask them: is this boring? Which part? Which sentence?

How can you be Unboring?

- For starters, be concise. Stay away from generalizations and platitudes.

- Include vivid details. Use the memorable punchlines you have thought of.
- Spend time to come up with the "hook" for your essay and memorable opening and ending lines.
- Read great fiction. It will make you a less boring writer (and a less boring person).

3. Avoid big words

There are exactly two reasons why you would use elephantine, gargantuan words in tortuously serpentine sentences:

a. either you have a prolific vocabulary and want to show it off, or
b. you have a sparse vocabulary and want to hide it.

I suggest that you hide your impressive vocabulary or show off your meager one, as the case may be. Your prose has to flow. Big words are the boulders that stagnate - and may even crash - your essay.

4. Avoid clichés

Clichés are unoriginal. Be original. Clichés crop up when you are lazy. Don't be lazy. If you are lazy you are not likely to be rich and famous. And we know how colleges feel about that.

Get help from others in spotting clichés if you aren't good at finding them.

A phrase may be clichéd but so may a thoughts or even the theme. Guard especially against clichéd themes. Please don't kill off your pet. Please don't swear to work tirelessly for the poor. Unless, that is, you can tell it originally and memorably. This is easier said than done so proceed with caution *[double cliché alert!]*

5. **Avoid exaggerations and sensationalism**

People often try to substitute exaggerations to force something to appear meaningful and memorable. It never works. Much like boring, unoriginal writing, exaggerations creep in when you are lazy. It takes time to come up with memorable thoughts and expressions. Spend the time.

6. **Don't be tone deaf**

Don't let your tone be too informal or too formal. Try not to talk to the reader like they are your best friend. Cuss words and colorful language are best avoided. Don't talk to them like you are addressing the Queen of England either. Extremely formal language will also keep you from making that connection.

7. **Avoid careless mistakes**

Your essay must not give the impression that you need to attend Derek Zoolander's "School for Children Who Can't Read Good"[4].

The is the easiest of the avoidable sins to avoid and yet, the admissions officer's life is full of essays with grammatical and spelling mistakes. Here are some tips for flaw-free prose:

- Put it on paper. Print your essay and read it on paper. Repeat often as you revise.
- Revise safely. Even after you think you are done, you will think of some small thing and revise a paragraph. Proof read the whole essay *every time* you do a revision, even a minor one. Run spell check

---

[4] From the movie Zoolander (Paramount Pictures – 2001)

every time you revise. Mistakes creep in even on the smallest edits.
- Get proof-readers. After some time you will stop seeing even obvious flaws in your writing. Have others proof-read your essay.
- Count the words. Make sure your word count is correct – you don't want to find out you are over the limit 15 minutes before the submission deadline.

Here is a small example of polishing up prose from this very book: the chapter titled "The Three Things Colleges Really Want" has about 400 words and I have re-read and revised it over 25 times.

12. What Got Me into MIT

As a 17-year-old writing my college essay for MIT, here is what I had to work with:

- I loved Mathematics and was very good at it; I also loved literature, creative writing, and science.
- I had good grades and test scores.
- I was fairly good in sports, especially tennis.
- I did not know what I wanted to be.
- I did know I wanted to study Mathematics.
- I wanted to win the Nobel prize for Mathematics (I did not know there was no such thing).
- Beyond sports, my extracurricular activities were few: a couple of school plays and the obligatory clubs. No contest wins, no science prizes, no debate team trophies, no meaningful volunteer experience.
- At the time of applying, I was working fulltime as a (very young) Math teacher at a local high school.

My Story Arc
My initial story arc was a laundry list of every subject I loved. Thanks to word limits, I realized that my interest and achievements in Mathematics had to be the main plot, capped by my experience as a 17-year-old teaching Math to 16-year-olds.

Draft #1: The Sad Lot of School Teachers
My first draft was all about the tragically underappreciated life of school teachers as seen by a caring (and dashing)

young outsider. It was my firsthand view of the unfairness of life and society towards the people who shape future generations. It was also melodramatic, self-indulgent, and boring. It showed me less as a brilliant Mathematician-to-be and more as a smug social commentator who had recently learned 3000 words for SAT Verbal and just discovered Dostoevsky.

Draft #2: My life as a Teacher
My next draft focused on my life as a precocious Math teacher, and how my love of Mathematics and zero generation gap with my students made me a rather good teacher. It was a decent essay with interesting anecdotes and evidence of self-motivation: I had applied for a full time teaching job of my own choice and had become a dedicated and respected teacher. The essay spotlighted my potential as a (self-proclaimed) Math whiz and a young leader. But I didn't think it hooked the reader. If I didn't *have* to read it, would I read it and love it? No.

Draft #3: The Job Interview
When I pruned away at my tolerably good second draft, one incident emerged from the debris: my interview for the post of a Mathematics teacher.

After an initial phone screening for the job, I went for an in-person interview. The principal talked to me for a few minutes and then told me their senior Math teacher was absent that day and so could not see me. I thought the interview was over but she said it would be great if I could substitute for him that morning. So 10 minutes into the interview process, I was standing in front of a bunch of grinning 10th graders (who I later discovered were the "troublemaker section").

I asked them what topic they were studying that week, and the answer came: "we don't know" *[general laughter]*. I asked to see their textbooks and they said "we don't have any" [*more laughter*].

So I decided to paint them a (verbal) picture. They may not be terribly interested in Advanced Math, but I was sure they were interested in big brand US colleges, the Wall Street lifestyle, and exotic Italian cars. So by way of introducing myself, I talked to them about the college application process that I was in the midst of. I spoke about what it takes to get into a great college, how a Harvard degree means you get hired straightaway at a big Wall Street firm, the six-figure salary at age 22, and how you get your first Ferrari before your 26th birthday. It all comes down, I told them, to doing brilliantly in your SATs, Subject SATs, and "core" school subjects. "And the single most important subject by far is Mathematics", I concluded. If they wanted their Harvard's and their Ferrari's, they needed to ace Math.

There was a dead silence. Then one kid stood up and said: "sir, I can go get textbooks from the section next door". I nodded. In a few minutes we started our lesson.

What I did not know was that the principal and the "absent" Math teacher were standing outside the door secretly listening in. They knew I knew Math. They wanted to see if I knew how to handle their rowdiest boys. This (as I found out after I got the job) *was* my interview.

The story of that "interview" became the essay that got me into MIT and many other colleges – where others with similar grades and better extracurricular activities did not get in.

Why this Essay Won
1. I was good at Physics, Chemistry, Biology, English Literature, and Mathematics. But I chose to highlight one subject, one passion.

2. I could have exaggerated my "decent" sports, extracurricular, and volunteer experience but I didn't. I focused on *one* exceptional non-academic experience: my job as a high school teacher at 17.
3. My theme hook was a single unique event: an unconventional job interview in which I shone. I whittled down months of teaching and years of interest in Mathematics to ONE hour.
4. I showed MIT how I took my love of Math farther than most 17-year-olds, and how I discovered my love of teaching in the process. If Mathematics had had a Nobel Prize, I would have won it[5]. How can an admissions officer reject that?

---

[5] Realistically, I wasn't going to win the Fields Medal (the "Nobel prize" for Math) but I think I would have been highly rated on Rate My Professors.

13. Essay: The Activist Who Spoke Too Much

In this and the next several chapters you will review the before and after versions of several personal statements. These essays come from actual college applications, though in most cases applicant names, locations, colleges, and programs, etc., have been changed and other small edits made.

Read each essay's original version and form your opinion of its content, theme, and style. Note the problems: clichés, boring passages, lack of brevity, careless mistakes. See the "first impressions" I had. Then read the final revision. Why is it better? Is it good enough?

For you to make all the mistakes and all the recoveries made by these applicants will take you a long time. Learn from their flaws, see their improvements, and save time.

Summary
Target: Undergraduate Admissions
Prompt: Tell us about a personal quality, talent, accomplishment, contribution or experience that is important to you.

Initial Draft
At one point in life, I could not differentiate myself from a Starbucks barista. I brought what seemed to be my hundredth coffee round to Congressman Rick Harding's office and stumbled into a familiar quandary. As an intern

in an office with such an impressive myriad of public officials, I typically kept my head down and completed assigned tasks. I often found myself coveting to interrupt heated discussions held in the office, but feared the consequences that would result from speaking out of turn. However, in this particular incident, my superiors were engaged in a heated dispute regarding my own school district. My direct supervisor was arguing in favor of expanding the campaign into local high schools, while her opponent argued the time and monetary repercussions of doing so.

I distinctly recall hearing: "The ones who want to get involved in the campaign will get involved. Otherwise, it's just a waste of time and money getting the attention of kids who can't vote."

"You'd be surprised how much some of these kids can do. I know for a fact that Ray Calderone has already expanded his campaign into my high school."

Everyone sitting down turned to look at me, as I slowly realized that these words had just come out of my very own mouth. I flinched at my inability to keep my mouth shut, and awaited my supervisors disapproving glare.
But it never came.

Rather, the head of the Congressman's campaign perused my interruption and replied, "Interesting point. And who are you?" I guilty introduced myself and he invited me take a seat on the table. What I did not realize then was that this interruption would later serve as the basis of my political career.

My coffee days were over, and I was given a permanent spot on the discussion table. As I became more confident in voicing my opinions, I saw myself develop from the quiet student intern filing papers in the corner to an active participant in these discussions. I became invested in my internship and more aware of issues surrounding the 12th district.

Working with other like-minded individuals in the office as an intern soon developed into a fellowship where I had the opportunity to lead discussions and create event content. I was later promoted to one of the Heads of Student Recruitment at the office, where I visited high schools and encouraged students to become involved with the campaign for Congressman Harding's re-election. When students realized that their involvement could potentially change policies such as university tuition hikes, they quickly became interested in helping the campaign. With the diligence of every volunteer and employee on the campaign, Congressman Harding was re-elected by an exceptional 2.5%. The Congressman himself thanked the Student Fellows for their efforts, reiterating the significance of a victory in such a tight race.

I cannot articulate the extent of effect that my experience with Congressman Harding's office has had on me. I had the opportunity to learn and apply crucial skills in leadership, diligence, and situation control. But more than that, I learned the significance of speaking up. If I had not interrupted in that single discussion, it is possible that many of precincts covered by student volunteers would not have been reached. My voice had the ability to help change the fate of the 12th district, but even more importantly, had the ability to change me.

First Impressions
- Good focus and theme hook: I especially like the coffee construct.
- Opening Hook: a somewhat desperate attempt at a cute opening.
- *"perused my interruption"*. That means, he *read* your interruption?! Confusing.

- *"I guilty introduced myself"*. Why would you introduce yourself guiltily?
- *"reiterating the significance of a victory in such a tight race"*. You mean the significance of *their contribution* in such a tight race.
- Your essay has several over the top moments that probably never happened. For example, it is hard to believe you *"flinched"* at your *"inability to keep my mouth shut"*. (I flinched reading that.)
- *"I cannot articulate the extent of effect that my experience with Congressman Harding's office has had on me"*. Clearly.
- Overall: A good first draft and very good theme hook. Much work still needed to make it more impactful and memorable.

Final Version

My greatest accomplishment stems from a cup of coffee.

It was a non-fat caramel latte to be exact, and it was among several other cups which I had brought to Congressman Rick Harding's meeting during my 27th coffee-carrier round to his office.

As an intern in an office filled with prestigious public officials, I typically kept my head down and completed assigned tasks. As I passed out coffee cups, I sometimes wanted to interject in discussions held in the office, but feared the consequences of speaking out of turn. However, during one particular coffee round, I overheard a heated dispute regarding my own school district. My supervisor was arguing in favor of expanding the campaign into local high schools, while her opponent debated against it.

I recall hearing: "the ones who want to get involved in the campaign will get involved. Otherwise, it's just a waste of time and money getting the attention of kids who can't vote."

I set down the caramel latte with conviction: "you'd be surprised what influence these kids can have. Congressman Calderone is already utilizing their potential and has expanded his campaign into my high school."

Every head in the room turned in my direction and I nervously awaited my supervisor's disapproving glare. It never came.

Instead, the head of the Congressman's campaign, replied, "Interesting point. And who are you?" I introduced myself and he invited me take a seat on the table. What I did not realize then was that my coffee serving days were over: this interruption would serve as the start of my political career.

I was given a permanent seat at the discussion table. As I became more confident in voicing my opinions, I developed from the quiet intern filing papers in the corner to an active participant in these discussions. I became invested in my internship and more aware of issues surrounding the 17th district.

Working with other like-minded individuals in the office as an intern soon developed into a fellowship where I had the opportunity to lead discussions and create event content. I was later promoted to one of the Heads of Student Recruitment at the office, where I visited high schools and encouraged students to become involved with the campaign for Congressman Harding's re-election. When students realized that they had potential to influence policies, they quickly became interested in joining our campaign. With the diligence of every volunteer and employee on the campaign, Congressman Harding was re-elected by an exceptional 2.5%. The Congressman thanked the Student Fellows for their efforts, reiterating the significance of victory in such a tight race.

I cannot overstate what my experience at Congressman Harding's office meant to me. I learned leadership and situation control. But more than that, I learned to speak up. If I had not interrupted that single discussion, it is possible that many precincts covered by student volunteers would not have been reached. I would not have been able to help students find their calling in politics. My interruption helped change the fate of the 17th district. Just as importantly it helped change me.

It took 27 rounds of coffee to find my voice, but it was worth the wait.

14. Essay: The Dentist Who Hated Bugs Bunny

Summary
Target: Undergraduate admissions (pre-medical major)
Prompt: Some students have a background, identity, interest, or talent that is so meaningful they believe their application would be incomplete without it. If this sounds like you, then please share your story.

Initial Draft
"Bugs Bunny", the adored American cartoon character, brings up one of the most emotionally scarring experiences of my life. The distinct protrusion of my upper incisors gave me the nickname that haunted me for years in school. Not only did it make me self-conscious but somehow made me feel less than normal. So from an early age, I was well aware of the importance of having proper dental treatments. With maturity, one learns to look at the broader picture in life; its not merely the aesthetic aspect of dental care which needs to be reinforced but rather the simple yet misunderstood fact that dental care can literally become a matter of life and death. Improved oral hygiene is the gateway to improved overall health, a fact disregarded by the vast majority of the population.

My interest in pursuing a career in the health care industry was instilled at quite an early age as my parents wished for me to become a physician. "What do you want to be when you grow up?" - a question I have been asked multiple times but seldom have a satisfactory response to. The summer of 2005, however, helped put things into perspective. I woke up to intense shouting outside my bedroom, to find out that my cousin had been in a horrible car crash. Upon arrival to the ER, I came face to face with the horror of what had occurred. My cousin's jaw had been crushed. Fortunately, he survived but was severely disfigured. The events following his recovery proved crucial for the both of us: my intimate exposure to the art of dentistry and oral surgery contributed significantly to my affinity towards the profession. The skillful manner in which the surgeon attempted to piece back the broken teeth, the shattered jawline and bone fragments had drawn me in completely. It became the pivotal factor in my decision to pursue a career in dentistry.

I was mostly torn between medicine and dentistry, therefore, opted to pursue pure sciences in school. Since high school, I have volunteered at a number of hospitals and social benefit programs ranging from the charity run kidney transplant hospital, flood relief camp for victims, to teaching and educating poor kids. The most pivotal factor in my decision to pursue dentistry came about after discovering that people with oral cancers believed that it was a temporary infection that would heal itself. The absurdity of the event made me much more interested in dentistry, thus laying the foundations of a career in dentistry.

The state of the dental industry in Sri Lanka was lacking qualified and professional dentists. Clinics in Sri Lanka provide no dental plans for low-income families. Lack of dental care awareness not only worsens people's health, but delayed dental care incurs higher bills later on. This vicious cycle is quite prevalent in my society, especially within poor communities. The high costs of undergoing dental treatments is a major deterrent for the poor people of Sri Lanka, and over the years, has culminated into a societal norm of ignoring dental care altogether. A quick scan of the cross sectional population confirms this fact – majority of the population in Sri Lanka has discolored and deformed teeth. The use of the modern toothbrush is seen as a luxury rather than a necessity. People still use 'Miswak', a primitive wooden piece used instead of the toothbrush. Clearly, the need for public awareness and education regarding the need for dental care is required.

Entering college in New York turned out to be a culture shock I did not expect. My new life in a city thousands of miles away from home caused me to sideline academics and become complacent; my scores plummeted and it was not until start of junior year when I contained myself and began focusing on what matters. My grades improved and I was awarded a position on the Dean's List for two consecutive semesters. It bolstered my confidence and reminded me that hard work and perseverance pays off.

Post graduation work emboldened my dental goals indefinitely. During my time working for Dr. Fernando in Colombo, I realized how a simple denture replacement could instantly improve quality of life. Seeing patients walk in with severe pain but leaving pain-free, with a new outlook on life, moved me dramatically. It allowed them to live a normal life, eat the foods they love and talk properly. Such an impact of a relatively simple procedure is a stark reminder of the enormous benefits of having accessible dental care.

Dentistry truly is the perfect career for me. It's a long-term commitment to serving communities through constant learning and skillful dexterity to prevent my patients from the hardships I endured growing up. It will allow me to showcase my passion for the betterment of the society, manipulate science and technology to improve patient health, manage pain and one day run a clinic providing free care. As an aspiring dentist, this career provides the most stimulating opportunity to revolutionize dental care by spreading awareness, and making it accessible for all.

I am truly confident that I possess the required capabilities and skills to undergo the rigorous academic challenges I shall face in dental school. My voluntary work involved dealing with people of different backgrounds and statuses, further polishing my leadership and communication skills. The combination of learned skills, perseverance, and the desire to help others makes me the exceptional candidate for dental school.

First Impressions
- Opening: The reference to Bugs Bunny is arresting but the hyperbole *"one of the most emotionally scarring experience"* is an obvious exaggeration.
- Your experiences and anecdotes – Sri Lanka, NYC, etc. – are varied and interesting but they are not delivered in an interesting way. For starters, your sentences run on forever at times. You need to compartmentalize your thoughts.
- *"...its not merely the aesthetic aspect"*. Learn the difference between it's and its.
- At 900+ words, this is an extremely long piece.
- The ending, if one has the patience to reach it, is unremarkable.

Final Version
Of True Love & Shameless Greed

True to the stereotype, my South Asian parents always wanted me to become a physician. Until July 2005, it was clear that their passion for my future career outpaced my desire for the medical profession. My one concession to their dream was to pursue the sciences in middle school. I found (to their joy and my surprise) that I rather enjoyed both biology and chemistry.

Then came a midsummer night in 2005. I woke to chaotic shouting outside my bedroom to find that my cousin had been in a car crash. He had survived; but his jaw had been crushed. Witnessing his recovery was my first exposure to the art of dentistry and oral surgery. The skill with which the surgeon almost magically pieced back the broken teeth, the shattered jawline, and bone fragments; the reverence, awe and gratitude with which this alchemy was received by my family and friends; the unexpected lease on an un-disfigured life that my cousin received – all combined to form a certainty in my mind. I was 13, I was nearly two decades away from a DMD, and I had just become the dentist I was meant to be.

Going from inspiration to action, I started volunteer work during high school at various medical and dental clinics in Colombo. I assisted Dr. Fernando in his clinic the summer before college. An exceptional orthodontist, he and his staff helped me understand the art and science of patient care, of obsessive attention to exceptional quality. But amid the inspiring care, I noticed that patients from impoverished communities rarely visited us. I became privy to the reality that dental care is regarded as an optional luxury rather than a necessity. Later, my work at Colombo University Hospital's dental clinic again showed me how expensive and inaccessible good dental care is in Sri Lanka.

Oral hygiene is the gateway to improved overall health. Between low awareness and high cost, entire communities in Sri Lanka are at risk for poor quality of life at best and life threatening diseases at worst. A systemic change is long overdue and I hoped to one day be this change. More determined than ever to pursue Dentistry, the light of true love in my heart, I came to college in the US. Whereupon I too found that the path of true love never does run smooth.

A new life, a new college, a new country, and New York – it was a culture shock of the best kind... and the worst. Penduluming between chronic homesickness and newfound independence, my academic performance dipped. It was not until junior year that I focused once again on what had mattered most to me since I turned 13. Infatuations gave way to enduring love, and my grades improved, my resolve returned, my name made the Dean's List. I also started working with NJCares, putting in 250 hours of community service and getting a better understanding of my new community. I will avoid the cliché of stating how it "improved my communication and leadership skills" and say instead that friendships were born, connections were made, the value of long lasting relationships was realized. In training for The Life Dental, I could do worse.

The fall and rise of Dr. Fernando, DMD, behind me, I focused next on getting more work experience in a clinical setting. As I prepared for the admissions test, I rejoined Dr. Fernando's team in Colombo. The time spent in his operating room helped me appreciate afresh the art of dentistry expanding my interest into a devout ambition: each orthodontic placement was so carefully assessed and tweaked, minor changes producing masterpieces of fit and comfort. A profoundly thankful patient at the end of each procedure was addictively rewarding for us. I must confess I anticipated each patient's reaction with something approaching greed. The gratitude and respect of the patients added as much to my love of my chosen profession as the medical genius of the doctor.

And so, I offer your college my work experience and my academic commitment, my admission test score and my coursework. I also offer my love for the wizardry of dental surgery and my hope for changing the reach of dental care across low income communities – as much in New York as in Colombo.

And finally, I bring to you my unabashed greed for the smiling gratitude of my patients.

15. Essay: The Student and the Social Contract

Summary
Target: Undergraduate Admissions
Prompt: Reflect on a time when you challenged a belief or idea. What prompted you to act? Would you make the same decision again?

Initial Draft
On November 2nd, Senator Ben Wickham tapped me on the shoulder in the United Democratic Office and asked me my name, explaining that he had seen me on a number of campaigns in the area. I stared at him as we shook hands, dumbfounded that one of the most recognized elected officials in the state of California knew of my existence.

The venture into politics that led me to this point began months earlier with a heated dispute between a history teacher and I who recommended me *The Social Contract* by the philosopher Rousseau. He claimed that my generation was ignorant of the duties we were obligated to perform as citizens, particularly participation in society and local government. I argued that many students engaged in leadership roles, but after speeding through the text, quickly realized that he was correct in his accusation. While my involvements in activities such as Student Government were impressive, they did not exemplify any form of political awareness or activism: I was ultimately benefiting from a society to which I did not give back.

Determined to be the change I sought to see around me, I was compelled to volunteer in my community. I applied and was accepted to a competitive student internship for Senator Wickham's office, which became the jumpstart of my political student career. Using confidence, interpersonal skills, and enthusiasm to make connections in the office, I was offered opportunities under various mentors where my eyes were opened to a whole new world of policies and bills.

I quickly learned about the framework of our government, and became well acquainted with more local elected officials, including members of the district school board and city council. I sat in on meetings that I could have only dreamed of as a student, and saw my academic lessons spring to life in council and committee meetings. Fueled by this political experience, I was prompted to apply to become a City Poll Worker for the November election, and later accept a job offer to the United Democratic Campaign office, where I had the opportunity to meet the Senator.

Eventually, I brought this enthusiasm with me to my own extracurricular activities and joined a competitive civics team, "We the People," where I traveled to Washington D.C and had the opportunity to sit in court cases at both the US Military Court of Appeals and the Supreme Court. It seemed unreal and almost magical that only a year ago I was just another member on the board of student government and now I was sitting in the highest form of court in America.

Becoming involved with my local government has broadened my horizons and galvanized me to become an active participant in my community. My experiences and accomplishments in politics have paved the road to my college and career paths, where I aim to continue to be the difference I hope to see around me.

The challenge that my history teacher provided to me two years ago continues to drive me to accomplish new feats, and pushes my limits further each and everyday. I would indefinitely make the same decisions over again if faced with this situation and others. While the battle to challenge the stereotype of politically stunted generation was both exhausting and demanding, it was nonetheless incredibly rewarding.

First Impressions
- The events you focus on have the makings of a very compelling story. I like the challenge with the history teacher. But the narrative veers between stilted prose and melodramatic emotions.
- You need to dampen the hyperbole: *"I stared at him as we shook hands, dumbfounded that... [he] knew of my existence"*. Really? Dumbfounded?
- *"Using confidence, interpersonal skills, and enthusiasm to make connections in the office, I was offered opportunities under various mentors where my eyes were opened to a whole new world of policies and bills"*: even in a corporate resume this would be dry and boring. In a college essay, it has no place at all.
- *"...and pushes my limits further each and everyday"*: Not each and everyday, surely [and it's *every day*]. Lose the exaggerations.
- Ending: No hook, nothing memorable. You need to echo back your history teachers challenge in a more colorful manner.

Final Version
"Your generation is totally ignorant of your duties as citizens," said my 10th grade history teacher. "I suggest you pay special attention as you read Rousseau's *The Social*

Contract. It may wake a few of you up. But frankly I doubt if any of you can be bothered to get involved".

I argued that many students were engaged in leadership roles as well as volunteer activities.

He shook his head: "I don't mean college application fodder. I mean real activism. You kids are just not involved in society."

Reading *The Social Contract*, I realized that despite my involvements in activities such as Student Government, I did not show any political awareness or activism: shaping and governing the society that benefited me was a responsibility I was not living up to. I agreed with my teacher that I needed to be more involved. I disagreed that I would never be bothered to get involved. Both my contrition at realizing my apathy and my indignation at his belief that it was an incurable apathy prompted me to act.

I applied and was accepted to a competitive student internship for Senator Ben Wickham's office. Working with other like-minded students in the office as an intern developed into a fellowship where I had the opportunity to lead discussions and develop event content. I was offered opportunities under various mentors and was ushered into an un-trekked world of policies and bills.

I learned about the framework of our government, and worked with many local elected officials, including members of the district school board and city council. I sat in on legislative meetings and saw my academic lessons played out in council and committee meetings.

Becoming involved with my local government has galvanized me to also become an active participant in my school and my community. I joined a competitive civics team, "We the People," which led me to travel to Washington D.C. There I had the opportunity to sit in court cases at both the US Military Court of Appeals and the Supreme Court. It seemed surreal that only a year ago I was just another member of our student government and now I was sitting in the highest court in America.

The challenge that my history teacher thrust on me two years ago continues to drive me today. Earlier this year, I applied to be a City Poll Worker for the November 2014 election, and later accepted a job at the United Democratic Campaign office.

A few weeks ago, on November 2nd, Senator Ben Wickham tapped me on the shoulder in the United Democratic Office and asked me my name, explaining that he had seen me on a number of campaigns in the area. I stared back at him as we shook hands, perplexed how one of the most recognized elected officials in the state of California could possibly know of my existence. "It's so good to see young people like you involved in our community," he said.

The next week I told my history teacher what the senator had said to me.

"I proved you wrong," I said.

"I could not be happier", he replied.

16. Essay: The Economist Who Forgot Word Economy

Summary
Target/Prompt: Applying for need-based financial aid for an undergraduate program.

Initial Draft
In economics, theoretically the market system is the best allocating mechanism but practically it causes market failure similarly one might find the content of a course suitable for him but without any work experience one cannot decide if he has the motivation and the mindset to study a course. Working at DuPont I got an opportunity to observe many occupations, keeping in mind my skill set and passion for finance, a career in accountancy was the best fit for me. Whenever I see a billboard on the road I try interpreting the market strategy used by a firm and analyze how the advertisement can be improved, likewise in accounts we need to analyze financial data and make decisions based on it. I find analyzing fascinating as it arouses curiosity in me because it gives an insight into the data which helps us to decipher the hidden meaning of it.

    I did not have accounting in college but due to my interest, I use to go to my college library to study it. I found managerial accounting very interesting as it plays a critical role in decision making, controlling and improving the efficiency of the firm. It involves dealing with immense amount of detail and statistical data, which I find fascinating. My favorite part of mathematic is the statistics component because it challenges you; it cannot be solved using a simple procedure as one needs to think out of the box when dealing with it. I enjoy doing normal, binomial distributions, probabilities and calculus in mathematics as solving complex problems in mathematics and understanding the logic behind it intrigues me. Having studied Physics and Economics have helped me understand problems and construct arguments based on calculations, interpretation, quantitative and qualitative evidence as well as develop my analyzing and evaluating skills. Studying Psychology in A levels has helped me in understanding the role of human behavior in the business world and analyze my point of view from different perspectives.

A year ago I worked as an intern at DuPont with the team of Corian (brand of DuPont). This experience helped me in becoming more organized, managing time and meeting deadlines especially after summer vacations when I had to work after school and manage my extracurricular, school and internship assignments. Over time I proved my worth to the firm as I brought new clients independently and convinced many architects and fabricators to switch to Corian. Doing market research and giving presentations on various topics like "Reasons for low market share" gave me a deep insight into the corporate world and improve my communication skills and boosted my confidence. I was often praised by my colleges for my dedication and passion for working in a firm especially because I was the only non paid intern due to the fact I was not a university student. But for me not being paid didn't matter since the experience I gained was hundred folds more valuable.

I joined Dextor Financial Services as a member of the financial department but due to my performance I was offered an executive position of Vice President of

Communications just after two months. I was part of the team which introduced the first student run credit card in Pakistan, offering credit card services to all students of our college. My role in this project was to get vendors for our credit card and sponsors for our project. During the first two months I was successful in getting top large chain restaurant and outlets like Subway, Khaddi, Expresso and OPTP on board. A key part of my job was to bridge the communication gap between Orix, our executive team, our entity's departments, board of directors of Dextor corporate and the vendors. Apart from this I was leading other projects like our virtual stock exchange and the customer care department of our credit card. This helped me develop leadership skills and I learned how to influence and motivate my team. I was also doing the billing and managing the credit limit of the credit card. This helped me in enhancing my IT skills as I was using many conversion software to manage the transactions of the students and generate the bill. I had to pay a lot of attention to the slightest detail as I was dealing with a lot of statistical data and there was no room for error, helping me improve my eye for detail. Working in Dextor Financial Services helped me improve ability to work in groups as well as independently as I had to do some projects with a team while others independently.

First Impressions
- You are clearly passionate about Accounting, Economics, and Finance and have a lot to say about your interest. Unfortunately, you have too much to say. The essay has to be trimmed be to be effective.
- Beginning Hook: The opening paragraph is too verbose and dry to hook me in. Don't start with *"diverse scope of interest"*. It means nothing in

particular and it is not the best way to start the essay.
- You use the word interest FOUR times in the first three lines – not good and not memorable.
- You have a lot of experience which is great but it will be meaningless if you lose the reader.
- Ending: The essay just dwindles out without a memorable takeaway or parting thought.
- Overall, this looks like a detailed listing of experiences rather than a compelling story about your passions and interests how they motivated your work experience.

Final Version
Call me a finance geek, a number cruncher, or a natural-born accountant: where my friends wish to learn Java, I want to master the language of business: Accounting. Finance has always topped my scholastic interests and Mathematics has been my academic strength since Grade 1, but what really sparked my interest in Accounting, was my internship at Dupont. It helped me understand the role of accounting through the lens of the decision-making process of a corporation. I learnt how Make or Buy Analysis is used by firms to minimize costs by determining whether to produce or buy components. Furthermore, I learnt how accountants use techniques such as tax avoidance to minimize taxation and cost of production. This showed me that accountants are not book keepers but strategists invaluable to a firm's success. This is why I wish to pursue Accounting & Finance at an undergraduate level.

My current A-level subjects have given me a head start on the road to a degree in Accounting & Finance. Studying Physics and Mathematics has enhanced my ability to think analytically, to construct arguments based on qualitative and quantitative evidence and to understand the logic behind problems. These skills will assist me in interpreting and forecasting financial data, and building valuation models. Psychology, on the other hand, has helped me in understanding the way people think and make decisions. I read in an academic journal about a research in which the sales of jam bottles decreased when there were twenty-four brands of jam bottles displayed for selling as compared to when six bottles of jams were displayed. This defies economic theory which states consumers want more choice. However, Psychology explains that consumers were not able to make a decision due to cognitive overload. This will help me in understanding business strategies as well as the role of human behavior in the business world.

To get a deeper understanding of entrepreneurship, I became a part of the executive team of Dextor Financial Services and introduced a student-run credit card for the Dextor Community - the first of its kind in Bangladesh. I was able to apply concepts I learnt in economics like Game Theory in practical situations, such as when I was negotiating with sponsors, firms and vendors.

I interned at DuPont where I independently brought new clients to the firm and convinced architects to switch to DuPont Corian. Dealing with clients, conducting market research and giving presentations on topics such as 'Reasons for Low Market Share' gave me an insight into the corporate world and helped me improve my communication skills. Working at DuPont also helped me in improving my ability to work in groups as well as independently due to independent and team projects.

Besides this, I had the opportunity to intern at Dupont in the accounting department, where I was able to familiarize myself with the duties of a traditional accountant. I reconciled balance sheets, did data entry, processed invoices, learnt about auditing, and made account statements as well as fixed asset schedules and tax certificates. Moreover, I learnt that the applications of accounting are widespread. For example, I saw how Accounting and Marketing work together to monitor the ratio of marketing expenses to gross sales by using Ratio Analysis, making sure that the expenditure incurred by advertisements is affecting sales.

Studying in a global financial center like the United Kingdom is my dream and ambition. Its colleges offer some of the best undergraduate programs in Accounting and Finance. Its cultural diversity will enable me to learn from different people and prepare me better for a career in international finance. Studying in UK will also allow me to indulge my passion for football and finally experience my favorite premier league clubs in person. I will in turn give my scholastic and personal best to my college.

17. Essay: The Animal Lover with Attention Deficit

Summary
Target: Undergraduate Admissions
Prompt: Describe the world you come from — for example, your family, community or school — and tell us how your world has shaped your dreams and aspirations.

Initial Draft
One day, when I was 13 years old, I was at home with some of my friends and the doorbell rang. I answered the door and saw my neighbor Alec holding a baby dove with cuts all over one of its wings. He had brought it to me to ask if I could take care of it, because he knew that I loved helping animals. I had never had to care for an injured baby bird before, only healthy babies, or injured adults, so I wasn't really sure what to do. I looked up online of how to clean the birds' wounds, and since I had cared for baby doves before, I knew what to feed it. It took many days for the wound on his wing to heal, and after that I still had to teach him to fly. The attachment I had with this bird grew into a friendship, and I was more than happy to see him healthy and able to fly. Letting him go made me sad because I knew I would miss him, but I felt amazing because I knew I had really helped this birds' life.

When I was younger I really liked catching birds, butterflies, and lizards. My dad told me that he had tried making a bird trap with a box, stick, string, and bird food but that he was never able to catch anything. I took this as a challenge and decided to make one of those traps. I was so determined to catch a bird and promised myself I wouldn't give up until I did. I waited in my backyard with the trap for two days until I was finally able to catch a bird. If I set my mind to something, I am a very motivated person and I will not give up until I finish it.

Hide! Your parents are outside telling you to go home! The mean people are angry because they saw us playing in their yard! Look the UH guys are standing outside and counting their fruit! Well this is awkward because Ron just saw us taking the bird food from his bird feeder. There comes Alec on his bike again and he's holding a baby bird this time! Mary is eating rice without ketchup for once!! Ugh Cuddles just dug another hole under the fence. Let's play Gamecube or the item game! Is Martha putting ice in Lori's fish tank again? Ew Jenny just ate that gum off the ground! And of course Tiina has her net and is chasing birds, butterflies, and lizards as always! I don't think anyone could really be able to call this their average day, but this would be considered a pretty normal day on Carnelle Court.

My weird childhood has shaped me to become the outgoing and unique person that I am. I grew up around all sorts of people of different ethnicities and backgrounds but somehow we all got along really well right from the moment we met each other. My strongest and best friendships were the ones I made with the other kids who lived on my street starting when I moved here at age 4. I've always been someone who likes to go through with random ideas, and prove people wrong by doing anything that people tell me I can't. Most people always assumed that I was quiet and studious like most of the other Indian or Pakistani kids in my neighborhood. They had parents who made them spend all their time studying and doing homework. I'm thankful that I didn't grow up that way. Being half Indian and half Pakistani and growing up with parents who let me do what I enjoy doing has caused me to be a very open minded and accepting person.

First Impressions
- The opening is nice and appealing but the story arc of your aspiration from childhood to now is not at all clear. Just being in love with animals is not enough. You need to come across as someone who has done a lot with that passion.
- The overheard dialogues make the essay real and unique but need to be formatted and highlighted properly.
- There are two distinct themes brewing here: you as an animal lover and you as a contrarian who is always open to new ideas and adventures. The latter is not well formed at all.
- Ending: You skim over a potentially powerful narrative about your parent's cultural and national heritage. Develop this further.

Final Version

For 18 years my natural habitat has been Carnelle Court, the cul-de-sac where I grew up. Think United Nations meets the San Diego Zoo. Ethnicities: Bulgarian, Israeli, German, Peruvian, Chinese, Indian, Pakistani, Midwestern-American, Russian. Pets: butterflies, fish, chickens, dogs, bunnies, lizards, cats, birds, hamsters. My love of animals, of athletics, of garage startups, and of thriving on what's new, all trace back to Carnelle and what I did there.

If you had overheard my childhood, you wouldn't have missed the animal theme:

"Is Martha putting ice in Lori's fish tank again?!"
"Uh-oh: Ron just saw us taking food from his bird feeder."
"Look, Alec is holding a baby bird this time!"
"Here is Tina with her net, chasing lizards and butterflies."

Little wonder that at 6, when asked at pre-school graduation to complete the sentence, "When I grow up, I want to be...", I filled in "a person that takes care of pets." 12 years on, that's still the answer.

I once set up an aviary ER at home when my friend Alec brought a baby dove with cuts all over its wings. I looked up how to clean the bird's wounds, and what to feed it. Once the wounds had healed, I taught it to fly. Watching him fly was amazing even if seeing him fly away was sad.

Later, I discovered that the years spent chasing butterflies with friends had made me fleet-footed. I made Varsity Basketball and Track-&-Field, and went on to be second best in school history in long jump. Still later, I gave lessons to upcoming girl athletes in long and triple jump.

The Amazonian diversity of my neighborhood has meant that I am not merely open to new experiences and creatures – I seek them out, actively and fearlessly. Perhaps I find what unites us sooner than others do. Squiggles the lizard, my Bulgarian BFF, and I may have different notions of family ties, acceptable mates, and career aspirations but we all love a friendly face, summer afternoons, and lady-bugs. This quality – of seeking what's different yet finding what's familiar – traces back to one house in particular on my block: my home.

I am the product of a Pakistani Muslim athlete from Berkeley and an Indian Hindu astrophysicist from Caltech. Where a billion sub-continentals let a thin line infinitely divide them, my parents thrive on what makes them unique. In the multiple choices of my childhood, they always supported me when I stubbornly chose None Of The Above; also when I chose All Of The Above. More importantly, they never penciled in my choices for me. Their openness means that when people ask me if I'm Indian, Pakistani, or Californian, I reply "Yes." It also means that my comfort zone is everything outside of it. I seek my friends outside my culture, my experiences outside my past, my intended caregiving outside my genus.

Carnelle Court has made me the animal lover, entrepreneur, and athlete that I am and the veterinarian that I will be.

18. Essay: The Day Creativity Died

Summary

Target: Undergraduate Admissions, University of California

Prompt: Every person has a creative side, and it can be expressed in many ways: problem solving, original and innovative thinking, and artistically, to name a few. Describe how you express your creative side. [350 words limit]

Initial Draft

I express my creative side by creating. From the young age of 6, my passion about Legos had me putting hours into creating complex structures *from the thousands of bricks scattered around my floor.* Although I outgrew my joy of stacking bricks I found a new one in chess. Playing against thousands of people both online and tournaments each game I found a new way of checkmating them. My innovative gameplay helped me win first place in the Cal-State Chess Championship and the Age Level Tournament and a rating of 1500 *(Should I link the article about me setting record?).* I then started teaching chess to beginning and intermediate players. Creating a website called, chesstutoring.com, I taught both chess and math at my local library to kids ages 4-12. Each class I would make a multitude of chess puzzles and tactics for my students to fiddle with.

As the President of our chess club, in 2015, every Monday lunch I would think of fun ways to keep our members entertained; for example we had many games like "Bug house" and chess tower competitions. My unique thinking style also came in handy in 8th grade; after a couple courses in java I began using my creativity to make levels and games. After receiving a internship from a company called, in the summer of my junior year, I used the right side of my brain to design over a hundred levels for their game called, "DoggyRun." My (work on DoggyRun helped me receive another internship with the company. This summer I helped design over 50 quizzes for their latest app called, "bookquiz". My contribution to both apps led to me being recognized in the credits.

First Impressions
- You have a strong theme – Chess – but your storytelling lacks impact.
- Weak and almost trivially obvious opening sentence: *"I express my creative side by creating"*.
- There is no ending/conclusion in this essay. It's like you hit "submit" accidentally.
- There are no opening or closing hooks and nothing memorable in your essay. The admissions officer may remember that you were a young chess champion and that's about it. Both your opening gambit and your end game are weak.

Final Version
    I was a California State Junior Chess Champion at 8, started a chess tutoring business at 13, helped design one of the most popular puzzle games at 15, and was ranked in the top 50 (out of 10 million) in the strategy game, Hearthstone, at 17. You could say I owe my success to an

over-developed sense of strategy. I would instead thank my creative side.

Whether building or solving, magic happens when method meets madness. In chess, I studied endless opening gambits and end games. But my extraordinary success came from creating unheard of (at least by me and my opponents) move sequences. My chess play probably benefited from my earlier inventions in Lego universe. I almost never made the picture that was on the box, once modifying the Millennium Falcon into an Intergalactic burger joint. Lego blocks gave way to chess pieces but my "forget-the-box" thinking remained.

When I decided at 13 to start Chess-Squared, a tutoring business headquartered at our local library, the challenge was not beating opponents but making students fall in love with chess. So I gamified the teaching of chess, designing numerous chess puzzles, playing in the dark, and using candy as a reward so students happily accepted their homework.

Tutoring does not pay as well as software design so I got an internship at a game startup. I designed 50 levels for "Puppy Run" and earned a spot on the credits of a maze puzzle game with 2+ million downloads.

Predictably, my love of Chess and of game design led to my taking up Hearthstone, a card strategy eSport. Like chess, it's a canvas for creative strategizing. Creating unique decks and play styles, I rose to rank 36 out of 10 million US players. And, as with chess, I now tutor Hearthstone players on creative strategies.

You could say that my creative side is expressed in games –playing, designing, teaching them. But I don't see games as my only creative outlet. Chess-master, teacher, entrepreneur, or designer, ALL these roles give me creative outlet. For me, not being creative is a losing strategy.

19. Essay: The Student Who Forgot the Prompt

Summary
Target: Applying for Financial Aid
Prompt:
Please write a full statement in which you:
  a) explain why you are applying for financial support from the School.
  b) describe your academic interests.
  c) describe your relevant work experience (paid or unpaid) related to your programme of study.
  d) outline your career objectives and demonstrate how the studies you plan to undertake at LSE will contribute to these objectives.
  e) give details of the work you aim to pursue after completing your studies.
  f) if applicable, explain how it will contribute to the future development of your country.

[**Note:** Please do not exceed 750 words and please do not attach your CV. You may use a separate sheet if preferred, but you must include a word count at the top of the page.]

Initial Draft
I have a diverse set of interests in the field of social sciences ranging from Economics to Psychology. However, Finance has topped my scholastic interests. I am particularly interested in Corporate Finance as I enjoy

learning about valuation of shares and firms on the stock market. To pursue my interest, I started a project in my college called DFS Capital which serves as a student-run investment fund in Pakistan and proves to be a valuable teaching tool for students who want to learn about Investments and the Financial Markets. Furthermore, I find Managerial Accounting fascinating too, due to its significant role in strategic decisions making in the financial world.

While interning in the Accounting department of Dupont, I was able to get a better understanding of Corporate Finance and was able to familiarize myself with the duties of a traditional accountant. I reconciled balance sheets, did data entry, processed invoices, learned about auditing, and made account statements as well as fixed asset schedules and tax certificates. Moreover, I worked with the supply chain department and learnt how Supply Chain Accounting Techniques such as Target Costing and Quality Costing are used to optimize resources. As part of the executive team of Dextor Financial Services I introduced Dextor College Stock Exchange which is a project aimed to provide a simulation of a real Stock Exchange in our college. Moreover, I have interned at DuPont where I independently brought new clients to the firm and convinced many architects to switch to DuPont Corian. Dealing with clients, doing market research and giving various presentations on topics such as 'Reasons for Low Market Share' gave me a deep insight into the corporate world and helped me improve my communication skills. My work experience has helped me develop skills that make me stand out from my peers.

After completing my Masters Degree in Accounting and Finance I plan to work in the international banking sector. This allows me to develop a deep understanding about Capital Markets, Global Investment Management as well as build a strong base of experience in credit and corporate finance. Also it will enhance my communication, organizational and problem-solving skills. After this I shall return to Pakistan and become the President of one of the Financial Institution in the country as I aspire to be a leader. I aim to represent my company on The Pakistan Business Council to promote business awareness and encourage the development of multinationals in Pakistan. My leadership skills and ability to influence and motivate my peers will help me become the executive member of the Board. My career will provide me with the opportunity to work and build business relationships with multinational organizations, Government bodies of Pakistan and with global financial institutions. This will help me achieve my career objective of becoming the Governor of State Bank of Pakistan as I want to promote economic development in Pakistan and help the Government to achieve its macroeconomic objectives.

I want to pursue a degree at LSE is because it focuses on understanding problems through different perspectives. For example the 'LSE 100 course' allows a student to give explanation for arguments using different social sciences. In life ahead, this will help me understand different views of people, ultimately helping me to become a better team player and a better leader. Volunteering at the LSE volunteer center will allow me to meet new people and develop my communication skills as well as incorporate the will to make a difference inside me. LSE's cultural diversity will enable me to learn from different people and prepare me better for a career in international finance. The diverse alumni network of LSE allows me to increase my professional contacts as well as allows me to learn from their advice and experience. However I require financial support to pursue my degree at the LSE as my sole source of finance is my widowed mother who is near her retiring age. Instead of saving for healthcare for her old age she is willing to spend all her little saving on my college education. Moreover, I tried asking my relatives for a loan but they themselves are going through a financial crisis. Therefore, I request LSE to offer me a scholarship. In return I will give my scholastic and personal best to LSE and avail every opportunity to befriend, enrich and help shape it's community.

First Impressions
- Why you need financial aid is asked as the first/main question. You choose to give just a few lines to answering it *at the very end*. This should be the focus on your essay taken head-on at the start. So you need to reorder your points to focus on your financial need upfront, and emphasize your desire to go to LSE.
- You go on and on about internship experience but don't address **Prompt 'd'** – your career objectives - as fully and properly as you should.
- Try and guard against excessive, non-impactful words. You must eliminate over the top expressions or repetitive sentences and passages. For instance: *"The diverse alumni network of LSE allows me to increase my professional contacts as well as allows me to learn from their advice and experience"* can simply be *"LSE's diverse alumni network would be a huge asset to me on day one"*.
- Overall: you cover the topics sought in good detail, just not in the right order and with the right relative emphasis.

Final Version
Ever since I was 12, it has been my dream to study at LSE, and be counted one day as an LSE graduate. A few weeks

ago the admissions committee gave me permission to live my dream. And yet, without financial assistance, studying at LSE will never be a reality for me. My sole source of funding is my widowed mother who has singlehandedly cared for my younger brother and me these many years and who is near her retirement. Instead of saving for her old age she is willing to spend all her little savings on my college education. Even so we cannot afford more than a few thousand pounds per year. None of my relatives are financially so situated as to give more than small amounts towards my education.

I therefore beseech LSE to offer me a scholarship. In return, I promise my scholastic and personal best to LSE. I lay down in this statement my interests, experience, and ambitions, in hopes to show you the likely return on your investment in me.

While I have always been broadly interested in social sciences ranging from Economics to Psychology, Finance has always topped my scholastic passion. I am particularly interested in Corporate Finance and enjoy learning about valuation of shares on the stock market. Indeed, I started a project in my college called NFS Capital which serves as a one of a kind student-run investment fund in Pakistan and proves a valuable teaching tool for students about Investments and the Financial Markets. I also introduced Dextor College Stock Exchange, a project aimed to provide a simulation of a real Stock Exchange in our college.

My work experience has aided my understanding of Finance. While interning in the Accounting department at Dupont, I got a first hand view of Corporate Finance. I reconciled balance sheets, did data entry, processed invoices, learned about auditing, and made account statements as well as fixed asset schedules and tax certificates.

I also worked with the supply chain department and

learnt how Supply Chain Accounting Techniques such as Target Costing and Quality Costing are used to optimize resources. More recently, I interned at DuPont where I independently brought new clients to the firm and convinced many architects to switch to DuPont Corian. Dealing with clients, doing market research, giving various presentations on topics such as 'Reasons for Low Market Share' gave me insights into the corporate world.

My career objective is leadership in private financial sector leading ultimately to leadership in the public sector. After completing my Masters Degree in Accounting and Finance I plan to work in the international banking sector. This will allow me to develop expertise in Capital Markets, Global Investment Management as well as in credit and corporate finance.

After this, I plan to return to Pakistan and work towards becoming the chief executive of one of the private financial firms in Pakistan. I aim to represent my company on The Pakistan Business Council to promote business awareness and encourage multinational firms to expand in Pakistan. My career will provide me with the opportunity to build business relationships with multinational organizations, government bodies and global financial institutions. This will help me achieve my ultimate career objective of becoming the Governor of The State Bank of Pakistan. Our country needs strong institutions which in turn means capable, respected leaders with integrity and relevant experience. I believe I can be that for our premier Financial institution.

LSE's stellar academic reputation, its renowned faculty, its rigorous coursework, and gifted student body will be the best possible enablers for my ambition. Its diverse alumni network - captains of industry - would be a huge asset on day one. LSE's focus on understanding problems through different perspectives would be key to my career success.

For instance, the 'LSE 100 course' allows a student to give explanation for arguments using different social sciences. This will help me understand divergent views, ultimately helping me be a better leader. Volunteering at the LSE volunteer center will allow me to meet new people and foster the will to make a social impact, to go eventually from success to significance. LSE's cultural diversity will help me learn from different people, preparing me better for a career in international finance.

And yet all my ambitions are "such stuff as dreams are made on". The first step is an LSE education. You hold the means to make that possible. And I await your decision.

20. Essay: The Bookworm Who Ate SAT Word Lists

Summary

Target: Undergraduate Admissions

Prompt: Tell us about a personal quality, talent, accomplishment, contribution or experience that is important to you. What about this quality or accomplishment makes you proud and how does it relate to the person you are?

Initial Draft

To say that I'm a bookworm is a gross understatement. I won five consecutive "Read-A-thons" in elementary school. I am far more than a mere bookworm. Reading is my true love.

I could easily credit this love to the Harry Potter books; I've immensely enjoyed reading them and so much more. But my love of reading would not have developed, much less have branched out, had it not been for my parents.

I'm very lucky to be born into a family that highly values education and academic prowess. However, I'm even luckier to be born to parents who also value individuality. My parents have never prevented me from pursuing my own hobbies. In fact, they have encouraged me to embrace the things that I enjoy - pursuits I may have otherwise completely forsaken.

When the first of many stories popped into my head, my mother suggested I write them down. As I whipped out dozens of tales, she'd sit with me and illustrate them because unfortunately, I didn't inherit her artistic gene. Flash forward to the present and I write articles for magazines and blog for renowned companies. I've even become a prolific and award-winning writer of tasteful fanfiction. No pictures necessary.

When I was in first grade, my father bought a Pimsleur Mandarin Chinese audio set and the two of us would listen to nothing but the first chapter as he drove me to school. Though we didn't learn much past how to say "Excuse me! May I ask if you speak English?", the fun I had learning Mandarin with my dad prompted me to become a budding polyglot. Today, I'm proud to say that I'm (almost) fluent in Korean, Japanese, Spanish, French, and Hindi. Regrettably, my Mandarin still needs work.

My parents uncovered my penchant for writing and my lingual dexterity, but have done so much beyond that. They fueled my incessant curiosity, letting me see the world through inquisitive eyes. They instilled within me the invaluable traits of imagination, versatility, creativity, and perseverance, to name a precious few.

What my parents have done for me is nothing short of ineffable.

First Impressions
- Very well written draft. Good command of language. Very few grammatical mistakes.
- Too much focus on parents, not enough on applicant.
- At times wordy and verbose: needs to be more concise and punchy.
- Overall, a great effort; ready for final polishing.

Final Version

To say that I'm a bookworm is an understatement. I won five consecutive "Read-A-thons" in elementary school. I am far more than a bookworm. The love of books is my one true love.

I could easily credit this love to the Harry Potter books; I have enjoyed reading them immensely. But my love of reading and of writing would not have developed, much less have thrived, had it not been for my parents.

I'm very lucky to be born into a family that values intellect and learning. However, I'm even luckier to be born to parents who also value individuality. My parents have never prevented me from making my decisions, pursuing my interests and hobbies. In fact, they have encouraged me to embrace the things that I enjoy - pursuits I may have otherwise never taken up or quickly forsaken.

When the first of many stories popped into my head, my mother suggested I write it down. As I whipped out dozens of tales, she'd sit with me and illustrate them because unfortunately, I didn't inherit her artistic gene. Flash forward to the present and I write articles for magazines and blog for renowned companies. I've even become a prolific and award-winning writer of tasteful fanfiction. No pictures necessary.

When I was in first grade, my father bought a Pimsleur Mandarin Chinese audio set and the two of us would listen to nothing but the first chapter as he drove me to school. Though we didn't learn much past how to say "Excuse me! May I ask if you speak English?", the fun I had learning Mandarin with my dad prompted me to become a polyglot. Today, I'm proud to say that I'm (almost) fluent in Korean, Japanese, Spanish, French, and Hindi. Regrettably, my Mandarin still needs work.

My parents uncovered my love for writing and linguistics. They encouraged my curiosity, letting me see the world through inquisitive eyes and write it down with a confident hand. What my parents have done for me is nothing short of ineffable.

To ask what I can do for them in turn is a bit like asking, as the philosopher did (in mandarin): "How can a blade of grass repay the warmth of the summer sun?"

Reading and writing forever would be a good start.

21. Essay: The Boy Who Ignored Word Limits

Summary
Target: Undergraduate Admissions to Univ. of California
Prompt: What would you say is your greatest talent or skill? How have you developed and demonstrated that talent over time? [350 words or less]

Initial Draft

My greatest talent or skill is understanding and connecting with others and using that empathy to, either please or compete with them.

One of the major ways I used my ability to understand others was when teaching chess. Having been a student for both subjects I knew what my students wanted and didn't want. Having already been in their shoes I stayed away from the traditional boring methods of reading and studying play styles or equations. Just like how I had been discouraged by previous teachers because of the boring start I wanted to ensure my students became passionate about the subject so that all the homework and information wouldn't be as boring or discouraging to go over. My friendly teachings allowed my chess and math tutoring to continue for 4 years with multiple satisfied students and parents and allowed me to get a summer internship as an english and math teacher in Karachi, Pakistan.

My Urdu isn't very good but instead of holding me back my weak native tongue once again reminded me what it was like to be a student. My understanding of the students kept me speaking slow with simply vocabulary so all of them could keep up. Instead of only asking, "Any questions" I also went around the class finding the students who were staring off into space or taking longer than usual and stayed after class to reinforce concepts or explain problems to them. All of my students completed their summer classes with passing grades and the teaching program that I hesitated to volunteer for ended up teaching me the importance of empathy.

Another example would be being able to understand customer needs at the restaurant I work at called Spiceworks. My empathic thought allowed me to always know whenever a customer needed something extra. Whether it was giving out complimentary drinks or helping someone decided on what to order my service can all be tied back to me understanding what our customers wanted. My superb service lead to many five star reviews and maintained the great customer service standard of oe of the highest rated restaurant in San Francisco. My knack for understanding what others felt wasn't only useful when serving food but also was helpful when serving volleyballs.

I've played volleyball for 6 years now and feel that the mental aspect of the sport is equivalent if not more beneficial than the physical part. As a Captain of the Junior Varsity team when I was a sophomore and as a Co-Captain as junior during our last season my objective wasn't only to hit the ball as hard as I could to get a point but also to motivate my team to perform their very best as well.

Whether in practice or game I knew how bad it felt to make a mistake; being one of the team's leaders I made sure my team remained positive even after losing multiple points. During one of the closing games of our 2016 season we were faced against the (eventual) State Champions,

Saratoga High. I knew my team felt we were gonna lose so I made a deal with them; I told them if we win I'll give them all Gatorade for the next game. Our spirits were crushed after we lost the first game 23-25 so right before we went into our next game I said, "Listen up boys, the only thing that stands between us and victory .... Is defeat." The corny joke helped my team laugh again, have fun. We miraculously come out with a 3-2 win.

Empathy has been a big part of my success and achievements. *[604 words]*

First Impressions
- A solid first draft with some good anecdotes. I really liked the motivational speech to your teammates at the end.
- This is supposed to be a 350 word essay and your draft is over 600 words!
- Opening sentence: *"My greatest talent or skill..."* Choose one. The "or" lessens impact.
- Your transitions need to be smoother: your essay reads like a disconnected list of achievements.
- Your ending is bland and unmemorable.
- Be concise. Avoid 40+ word sentences like this gem: *"Just like how I had been discouraged by previous teachers because of the boring start I wanted to ensure my students became passionate about the subject so that all the homework and information wouldn't be as boring or discouraging to go over"*.

Final Version

My greatest talent is my empathy. My ability to put myself in another person's shoes lets me connect with them, mentor them, serve them, or lead them.

Whatever empathy I started life with, I have been developing it since 5 when I started playing chess.

Knowing what was going on in my opponent's head was, I realized, as important as what was happening on the board. My empathy made me a good strategist and a chess junior champion.

My teaching "career" developed my empathy further. When I started a chess tutoring service, I had to get inside my students' minds. Only then could I motivate them to excel in competitive chess. Later, I volunteered to teach English to underprivileged kids in Karachi. I thought my weak Urdu would be a handicap. But recalling how my cousins' rapid fire Urdu left me dumbfounded, showed me how my 3rd graders felt when speaking English. Feeling their shyness, made me a better teacher. Instead of merely asking, "any questions?" I went around to attend to disengaged students and stayed afterwards to tutor them. My empathy made me a much-loved teacher.

My empathy development (and demonstration) peaked when I was front-manager of a hugely popular Indian restaurant. I faced long lines and encountered all tastes, appetites, spice tolerances, finicky habits. I had only a few seconds to connect with customers and make them happy. My empathy earned us hundreds of 5-star reviews, lots of tips, and many loyal customers.

Most recently, my empathy helped me captain Meadowbrook's volleyball team. The game against the eventual 2016 NorCal Champions, Saratoga High, stands out for me. We were tied after two but heartbreakingly lost the third 25-23. My team was crushed. I knew instinctively that inspirational or angry words would not work. So I solemnly said: "Guys: the only thing that stands between us and victory..... is defeat." We all laughed, which was the needed medicine. We won 3-2.

Whatever I pursue in life, I know I will be called to lead and to serve. And I know my empathy will always serve me well.   [*348 words*]

22. Essay: We are All Chocolates

Essay Summary
Target: Undergraduate Admissions
Prompt: Write a letter to your future roommate.

Initial Draft
Dear future roommate,

I love food especially chocolate. I adore chocolate. Why? Because it comes in so many different shapes and sizes! When I am having a bad day, a mere bite of a chocolate bar can cheer me up. Some people like raisins in their chocolate; others prefer nuts, caramel, peanut butter, even jam! No two chocolate bars are the same. In other words, every chocolate bar is unique just like the person feasting on it.

Even though all chocolate bars are made from the same core ingredients, cocoa and vanilla, they taste different because of their supplementary ingredients, similarly, we are all made from flesh, bone and blood however it is our interests, passions, quirks and qualities that make us different from each other.

I enjoy traveling because I enjoy experiencing different cultures and meeting different people. I am an open minded individual who has developed a wide, varied palate.

I am a perfectionist by nature, but life has taught me to compromise. You see perfectionism comes in different shapes and sizes- just like chocolate bars. To me perfectionism is using what I have been given to the maximum i.e. a supportive family, a strong cultural background, a high moral ground and the determination to constantly improve.

    I greatly look forward to meeting you. I would have loved to give you a clichéd introduction to myself, but just look at some of the many qualities of chocolate!

Yours truly,

Munadil

First Impressions
- The whole chocolate theme comes across as trying desperately to be original and unboring but tells me very little about you (except that you believe in human diversity and, in a Forest Gump-ian way, liken it to a box of chocolates). It is not especially memorable.
- Shouldn't you be telling your roommate about your main interests and what sort of person you are rather than your philosophy of human-chocolate equivalence? After all, this is not really a letter for your roommate as much as a short essay for the admissions office.
- So how does this letter (which your roommate will never read) tell the admissions officer that you are marked for greatness in life?
- The ending line is completely cryptic: *"I greatly look forward to meeting you. I would have loved to give you a clichéd introduction to myself, but just look at some of the many qualities of chocolate!"* Why would anyone love to give a cliched introduction (did you mean a traditional introduction?). And how did the many

qualities of chocolate prevent you from giving a clichéd introduction?

Final Version

Dear Future Roommate:

My name is Munadil, Arabic for fighter or striver. Don't be alarmed. I may fight to get my point across (be prepared for healthy debates). I may fight over a good plate of Biryani (and other Indian culinary delights). And I fight for every point on the tennis court (did I mention that I am a tennis ace: we should definitely go hit a few rallies). But other than the whole fighting for excellence thing, I have the makings of a rather even-tempered, easy-going roommate who is a design geek.

My guilty pleasure is not YouTube pet videos on replay (which I kinda like), food crawls across Delhi (although I crave biryani 24/7), or Snapchatting my life (you must add me on Snapchat anyway). My idea of an hour of wanton pleasure is sketching or modeling industrial design concepts – from cars to toasters.

To my friends this seems boring (no selfie?!), possibly useless. But I intend to design an airplane that will revolutionize aviation (preferably before I turn 30). I am sure you will be glad that my most pleasurable past-time helps make that a little more likely every day and is guaranteed not to drive my roommate crazy.

I can't wait to show you my latest designs, play a set, and eat biryani with you!

Best,

Munadil

23. Essay: The Romantic Aeronautical Engineer

Summary
Target: Undergraduate Admissions
Prompt: What matters to you, and why? (Stanford) [100 to 250 words]

Initial Draft
Love. Love matters to me: The love my parents have given me ever since I took my first breath, the love my teachers have shown me throughout my prep, middle and high school life, and the love I have received from my peers- both friends and acquaintances. Love is not only something you can give, show or receive, it is something you can want as well.

I have always considered my interest in engineering as a relationship. It started quite a while ago, I can remember the six-year-old me drawing, designing and modeling aircraft, I can remember the eight year old me questioning myself, my friends, teachers, and parents about what makes an airplane fly? Why is it that an aircraft has the ability to remain airborne for such a long period of time? When I was ten I started to read books and watch documentaries on aircraft mechanisms, by the time I entered my teenage years I already knew more about air pressure, resistance and wingspan that a regular sixteen year old would.

Why? It's because I love aircraft, more specifically the engineering behind them, and I want my feelings to be reciprocated. That is where my motivation, determination and driving force to become one of the world's best aeronautical engineers come from.

Love brings with itself a potpourri of emotions and feelings. Desire, will, and passion are just some of the package's constituents. Science tells us that the universe is constantly in flux; it's what allows our friendships and our love to constantly shape us.

First Impressions

- Opening Hook: *"Love. Love matters to me… Love is not only something you can give, show or receive, it is something you can want as well"*. Well, I admit this opening paragraph would hook any reader, but I am not sure for the right reasons.
- *"Love brings with itself a potpourri of emotions and feelings. Desire, will, and passion are just some of the package's constituents. Science tells us that the universe is constantly in flux; it's what allows our friendships and our love to constantly shape us."* We all know love is complicated but this takes the notion to a different level. I don't have any idea what you are saying, and if I am an admissions officer, I am not motivated to try and get your drift.
- In the last sentence, when you say "it's what allows..." What do you mean by "it"? Science? The universe? The fact that the universe is in flux? Love? The package? Or one of the package's constituents?
- And do *"our friendships and our love"* need to be allowed *"to constantly shape us"*? And even if they do, how does that make you an appealing candidate for Stanford?

- This theme and essay will most likely have to be scrapped. You will need to come up with a new theme and story.

Final Version
"Remember that guy who gave up?"
"No."
"No one does."

The conversation replays in my head in an endless loop as I prepare to serve. I cannot take the pressure and break away from my motion. I turn around, face the fence, and reflect on my situation: I am a set and a break down against the top seed. What chance do I have of winning? How easy and understandable to simply go through the motions and then walk away from the arena.

I think of all the work that brought me to this moment. I had come to Kenya for an international tennis tournament. Competing at an international level is physically and mentally draining and you are rewarded with weeks of school work to catch up on. It is a sacrifice I have been making ever since I started to play competitive tennis and yet, I have never wavered in my commitment to court and classroom.

Now, at the point of checking out and walking away, I remind myself what matters most to me: that I never give up.

I turn around, straighten my shoulders, and face my opponent.

It matters not how I came to this moment. I cannot wish it away or run away from it. All that matters to me at this moment - and at all others to come - is that I commit to this moment body and soul.

24. Essay: Warning – Turbulence Ahead

Target: Undergraduate Admissions Supplemental Question
Prompt: Which department or program appeals to you at MIT and Why?

Initial Draft
To me, the world is an enormous airspace, where every aircraft's flight represents someone's life on Earth.

To live a long, successful life, I will need to design my aircraft accordingly. This is why I intend to major in Course 16 - aeronautical engineering. My life's ambition is creating an aircraft design that will revolutionize aviation and make me one of the most successful avgeek on the planet.

If the flight represents my life, then my job is to keep the aircraft constantly airborne. Because with the turbulence of uncertainty only with constant flight comes the growth of being constantly challenged

First Impressions
- I like the metaphor of life as airplane journey and all of us on our flights. But you need to use simpler, cleaner language to express yourself.
- The ending, for example, is fairly incomprehensible: *"If the flight represents my life, then my job is to keep the aircraft constantly airborne. Because with the turbulence of uncertainty only with*

constant flight comes the growth of being constantly challenged." No admissions officer will spend the time to decipher this.

Final Version

To me the world is a giant airspace and all our lives are airplane journeys of varying distances, durations, and destinations.

Since my life's ambition is to create an aircraft design that will revolutionize aviation, for me to have a happy flight I must learn to be a revolutionary aeronautical designer. This is why I must major in Course 16, aeronautical engineering, at MIT. There is, after all, no other place in the world that can better prepare me for my journey.

25. 'Why Our College' & Other Supplemental Essays

The supplemental essays always get left to the very end so there is no use in telling you not to leave them to the end. Here is what I will tell you:

1. Don't leave *reading* the questions till the end. You don't have to write up your responses, but read and think over the prompts well before submission day.
2. When you do read the questions, make a quick outline, jotting down some thoughts and ideas. This way, when you come back to them at the 11th hour, you will have something to work with.

There are two types of supplemental questions:

1. Tell us more about yourself
2. Why our college?

Type 1: Tell Us More About Yourself
This is typically an open-ended question asking you for anything else you wish the admissions officer to know. Here are a few things to keep in mind:

- Don't repeat what has already been covered in your main essays.

- You can choose to highlight an achievement which did not make it into your essay. Try not to list several minor successes or experiences.
- Take this chance to explain a glaring weakness in your application. Don't highlight a small deficiency or several weaknesses. It is best to explain **one** gaping hole in your application such as:
    a. poor grades in a particular year
    b. minimal volunteer or work experience
    c. low participation in sports and extracurricular activities

Some colleges have memorable "tell us about yourself" supplemental questions:

- *Tufts: What does #YOLO mean to you?*
- *Stanford: What matters to you, and why?*
- *U. of Chicago: What is square one, and can you actually go back to it?*
- *U. of Chicago: What's odd about odd numbers?*
- *Yale: You have been granted a free weekend next month. How will you spend it?"*

Be creative: the prompt demands it. But be smart as well: you should still highlight an unsung achievement or a major gap.

Type 2: Why Our College?
Here are a few things to keep in mind in answering this question:

1. Do your research. Look at the specific college/department website for your intended major/program/department (e.g., School of Engineering, Fine Arts Program, Biology Major,

etc.), not just for the main university. Simply showing that you have studied the college and department websites and gone on forums where alums and applicants are talking about the college gets you points.
2. Don't fake interest in professors and their research areas. If you are genuinely interested in a topic (say, AI or Russian Lit.) and have done independent research/projects on it, your application will bear this out and your familiarity with a professor's work will be understandable. Otherwise you will come across as desperate, fake, or weird.
3. Try not to copy paste portions of your college essays into these supplemental questions. No one wants to re-read your essay. You can re-use parts of a personal statement for another college in a supplementary essay, but make sure the recycled points connect nicely to the college at hand, its strengths, and its appeal to you.
4. Talk about the campus. If you have visited the college campus mention it. If not, say why the images and description of the campus appeal to you
5. Mention alums you know. Did an aunt, uncle or family friend go there? Describe your conversation with them on their college experience and why it made you excited about going there yourself.
6. Finally, make sure your answers are consistent with your essays and applications. Don't suddenly talk about your commitment to track and field because the college has a celebrated track and field tradition, unless you too have a fairly celebrated tradition.

Sample Essays: "Why Our College?"
Prompt: Tell us why you decided to apply to the University of Wisconsin, Madison.

[Here is a smart re-use of the essay you read in the chapter titled "The Animal Lover with Attention Deficit". The applicant has neatly connected her love of animal science, entrepreneurship, and athletics to the strengths of the college.]

There are three reasons why University of Wisconsin Madison is the college for me: my love of animals, my love of sports, and my love of entrepreneurship.

For 18 years my natural habitat has been Carnelle Court, my home street. Think United Nations meets the San Diego Zoo. Population: 51. Ethnicities: 13. Pets: Countless. My love of animals, of sports, of entrepreneurship, all traces back to Carnelle. When I was asked at my pre-school graduation to complete the sentence, "When I grow up, I want to be…", I filled in "a person that takes care of pets." 12 years on, that's still the answer. *UWM's top rated Animal Science undergraduate program is the biggest draw for me.*

At 14, I discovered that the years spent chasing butterflies had made me fleet-footed. I made Varsity Basketball and Track-&-Field, and went on to be second best in school history in long jump. Later, I gave lessons to upcoming girl athletes in long and triple jump. *UWM's amazing sports tradition – and especially its track and field team- is one of the main reasons for my application.*

The Amazonian diversity of my neighborhood has meant that I seek out new experiences, actively and fearlessly. This quality traces back to my parents, who thrived on what made them unique. In the multiple choices of my childhood, they always supported me when I chose None of the Above; they never penciled in my choices for me. Their openness means that my comfort zone is everything outside of it. I seek my college outside California, my friends outside my culture, my intended caregiving outside my genus.

It also means that entrepreneurship is my chosen vocation. My eventual startup will be in animal-care. UWM must therefore teach me not only Animal Science but also entrepreneurship. *Hence, the highly ranked Center for Entrepreneurship at the School of Business will have me a regular visitor.*

Carnelle Court has made me the animal lover, athlete, and multicultural expert that I am. UWM will make me the veterinarian and entrepreneur that I want to be.

Prompt: Tell us what draws you to Mount Holyoke College.

[Here is a concise but colorful listing of things that appeal to the student. It shows the applicant has done their homework via campus visits, talking to alums, etc. Short sentences are used to great effect. The ending resonates nicely with the listing in the essay body]

In order to show you why I am drawn to Mount Holyoke, let me draw you a literary mosaic of reasons which come together in my mind whenever I am asked "Why Mt. Holyoke?"

The amazing hands-on biology program. *The singing canoes.* The class entirely on marriage in literature. Boston. A flexible liberal arts experience. The fact that Emily Dickinson was an English alum. The nightly milk and cookies. A 9:1 student-teacher ratio. The Pre-vet club. Mountain day. The wonderful English program.

Mount Holyoke offers me a great liberal education which would indulge my love of literature and biology. That is what draws me to Mt Holyoke. That and the singing canoes.

26. A Word on Cheating: Don't

There are three common ways to cheat on college essays:
A. Making Stuff Up
B. Copying Stuff
C. Hiring a Writer
[D. All of the Above?]

Making Stuff Up
If you are going to hoodwink the admissions officer, you better do it perfectly. The admissions office at a competitive college has probably read more than a million essays since you were born (the larger public universities have seen a million just since you entered high school). Essays about leadership in imaginary extracurricular pursuits, work experience that is a work of fiction, tales of life-changing volunteerism that never happened, will probably not be consistent with other parts of your application. This will likely be detected. And you will likely be rejected.

Even if your untruths are not sniffed out, writing about something that is mostly non-existent will never feel as compelling as an essay about something that happened and that *you* feel strongly about.

Copying Stuff
Taking someone else's life story off the Internet and making it your own is dangerous business. First of all, you

are probably not the only one who read that great essay. Second, you will find it hard to make it consistent with the rest of your story. If you are willing to put in the time, effort, and craft to make it perfectly consistent, might I suggest you simply spend that energy in writing a good essay. While we are on the subject, don't copy one of your own high school essays. The effort you will spend trying (and failing) to fit it to a prompt and your overall application is not worth it.

Hiring a Writer

If you are a good writer, you will not hire a writer. If you are a bad writer it will show up in your grades (among other things) and your perfectly written essay will be inconsistent with the B's and C's in Language Arts. If the college gets any doubts about who actually wrote your essays, they will not take a chance.

This is not to say you can't get help from friends and family (and, yes, even experts) to improve your drafts, catch the poor grammar, or come up with that wow ending. But your essay must be your thoughts, your life, and, as much as possible, your words.

Missing the Point

The best thing about writing your college essays is the chance to review your life, purpose, and potential. This is not something you have ever done. Sadly, it is not something you will ever do again. Don't blow this one chance to look at yourself and describe what you see.

My Advice

Don't Cheat. No matter how much you want to go to a big name college, it's not worth it.

"A degree from MIT is a wonderful thing; but if you are not enough without it, you will never be enough with it."[6]

---

[6] Paraphrasing the great John Candy in "Cool Runnings" (Disney Pictures, 1993).

27. Theorem: Applying to College is Stress-free

"Happiness equals reality minus expectations."
- Tom Magliozzi, co-host of NPR's Car Talk & MIT alum

Hypothesis 1: Admission to a Top 25 College is a Virtual Lottery
For the vast majority of applicants getting into the top 25 US colleges is heavily against the odds.

When acceptance rates drop to 4% (Stanford), when you are 1 of 100,000 applicants to UCLA, getting in is a low probability game. You should certainly play this game: work hard to improve your odds, select your "stretch targets" wisely, apply to your dream college no matter the odds, and hope for the best. But don't confuse "hope to" with "expect to". No one ever bought a lottery ticket, stressed every moment until the results were announced, and cried for days because they expected to win. Neither should you.

Proposition: No More, No Less
Given Hypothesis 1, and before moving on with our proof, I want to highlight a simple reality about college admissions:

On the day you hear a great college accepted you, you will be *only* as good as you were the day before, *no more*.

On the day you hear a great college rejected you, you will be *just* as good as you were the day before, *no less*.

Hypothesis 2: Admission to a Top 200 College is a Virtual Certainty

Getting into one of the top 200 colleges in the US is virtually a certainty for most students. Many of them (51, actually, per US News and World Report 2017) have **acceptance rates above 75%**, including:

University	Rank	Accept Rate
Yeshiva University	66	80%
University of Iowa	82	81%
Indiana Univ. (Bloomington)	86	78%
Univ. of Colorado-Boulder	92	80%
Drexel University	96	75%
Auburn University	99	78%
University of Tennessee	103	76%
Iowa State University	111	87%
University of Utah	111	81%
University of Oklahoma	111	78%

[2017 US News & World Report: National Universities Ranking]

Other universities that rank in the top 100 with **acceptance rates above 50%** include:

University	Rank	Accept Rate
U. of Illinois Urbana-Champaign	44	66%
Penn State University	50	51%
University of Washington	54	53%
University of Georgia	56	53%
Purdue University	60	59%
University of Connecticut	60	53%

[2017 US News & World Report: National Universities Rankings]

If you really messed up in high school, you have junior (community) college to get you back on track and into one of the top 200 colleges (perhaps even one of the top 100).

As there are over 4000 degree colleges in America, this means you are guaranteed to attend one of the top 5% of colleges in America.

As there are over 40,000 colleges in the world (and as US universities monopolize the top of world rankings), this means you are guaranteed to attend a college among the top 0.5% in the world.

The Theorem: Applying to College is Stress-free
Given:
Admission to a top 25 college is a virtual lottery [Hypothesis 1].

Given:
Admission to a top 200 college is a virtual certainty [Hypothesis 2].

It follows:
> *For all applicants:*
>
> *who apply to good colleges with high acceptance rates*
>
> *AND*
>
> *who would not cry for days if they did not win a lottery,*
>
> **Applying to college is stress-free**

[QED]

The Equation
If you *expect* to get into a top-25 US college you will be stressed until the results come out and probably unhappy after they do.

If you expect to get into one of the top 200 colleges (whilst hoping for more), you will be stress-free until the results come out and happy thereafter.

The equation to remember when applying to college (and forever after) is:

Happiness = Reality - Expectations

28. The Greatest Finish Ever

We end where we began, by reflecting on what great colleges are looking for in you: the potential for fame and fortune. Or, more specifically, the self-motivation to succeed.

In case you have not figured it out already: college applications don't matter.

Only one thing matters. And it is not getting into (a) an Ivy League University, (b) a big brand name engineering program, (c) a Most Selective liberal arts college, or (d) a top 5 business school.

The only thing that matters is whether you are truly self-motivated.

Which brings us to our final story of self-motivation.

John Stephen Akhwari was a long distance runner who represented Tanzania in the 1968 Mexico City Olympics. During the marathon he fell, badly cut his knee, and dislocated the knee joint. Instead of quitting, he kept going.

As he neared the finish line, the small crowd that remained cheered him on.

He finished last among 57 competitors.

When asked why he had continued running even after he had no hope of medaling, he seemed surprised at the question. Then said: "*My country did not send me 5,000 miles to start the race. They sent me 5,000 miles to finish the race.*"

If you are not self-motivated, it does not matter what college you get into.

If you are self-motivated, it does not matter what college you get into.

Acknowledgments

To: my family for all their feedback and support, and for sharing my excitement; my friends for helping me choose the cover and improve what's inside; my cover designer, Omake, for being exceptionally talented (and exceptionally patient with all the revisions); Borislav for livening up the pages with his graphic art; all my reviewers for their feedback and testimonials; Jeff Brenzel for his sage advice; and, above all, Mariam, Sabina, Omer, Samar, Mujahid, Hammad, Anya, Mirha, Sahlik, and all the other college applicants who generously shared their essays so that their experience may benefit future applicants,

Thank You.

Umair

Preview: College Application Hacked – Part 2

"College Application Hacked - Part 2: Crafting a Winning College Application" will show you how to choose the right colleges, collect the necessary ingredients for a successful application, and compose a college application that will beat the *Acceptance Odds*.

You will learn about:
- Going deep vs. going wide
- The other GPA
- What you should have done in middle school (and how to make up for it now)
- Your high school *must-do* list
- Presenting extracurricular experience

You will also learn how to choose the best colleges that will love you back, as we cover:
- College rankings
- Department vs. institution ranking
- Acceptance rates
- ARI: The Acceptance-rate to Rank Index
- The "Public" Ivy's
- Women's colleges

To learn more, visit: www.collegeapplicationhacked.com

About the Author

Umair applied to and was accepted at Princeton, MIT (twice), Stanford (twice), Yale, Cornell, Dartmouth, Brown, and Carnegie Mellon. He received an SB in Math with Computer Science and an SM in Computer Engineering both from MIT.

As a tech entrepreneur in Silicon Valley, California, he co-founded SecretBuilders, an educational games startup and Folio3, a software development house. Through the SecretBuilders Summer Program, he has mentored over 120 students on college applications. He has spoken on entrepreneurship at various universities including U.C. Berkeley, Harvard, and MIT. He also counsels students on their career paths. You can reach Umair at **ukhan@alum.mit.edu**.

About Pi

In case you are interested, the author's golden-doodle dog featured on the back cover is named Pi, and was born (nearly) on Pi Day (3.14.16). Pi is currently attending vet school. Umair had nothing to do with his admission to vet school.

Index

A

acceptance rates, 114, 115, 116
ACT, 12
activism, 39, 64, 67
Activist, 51
aeronautical engineering, 104, 105
AI, 28, 108
alums, 108, 110
Amazon, 28
Animal Lover, 75, 109
apathy, 39, 67
application process, 29
Author, 122

B

Before and After, 40
Bobby Fischer, 27
Bookworm, 90
Boring, 42
Brainstormers, 24
brand name, 118
Brown, 8, 122
Bryn Mawr, 17
Bugs Bunny, 57, 60
business school, 118

C

careless mistakes, 42, 45, 51
Carnegie Mellon, 8, 122
Cheating, 111
chess, 27, 31, 32, 37, 80, 81, 82, 94, 96, 97
Chocolates, 98
Cliché, 42
Cool Runnings, 113
Copying, 111
Cornell, 8, 122
Creativity, 80
Cuss words, 45

D

Dartmouth, 8, 122
deadline, 30, 46
Disney, 113
Draft, 51, 57, 64, 69, 75, 80, 83, 90, 94, 98, 101, 104

E

Economist, 69
Education Technology, 9
Empathy, 96
Ending Hook, 35, 39
entrepreneur, 9, 79, 82, 110, 122
Equation, 116
exaggerations, 45
Expectations, 117
extracurricular, 10, 12, 27, 31, 47, 49, 65, 70, 107, 111

F

fame, 13, 14, 118
fellowships, 8
Financial Aid, 83
Fine Arts, 107
First Draft, 30, 33
fortune, 15, 118
freshman, 27, 29
Frodo, 29

G

Gandalf, 29
GPA, 12, 14, 29

H

Hamlet, 31
Happiness, 114, 117
Harry Potter, 23, 31, 90, 92
Harvard, 15, 17
Hobbit, 29
Hypothesis, 114, 115, 116

I

Influencers, 24
Internet, 111
interviews, 9
Ivy League, 8, 9, 118

J

James Herriot, 28
java, 32, 81
John Candy, 113
John Stephen Akhwari, 118

L

Language Arts, 112
lottery, 9, 114, 116
LSE, 40, 83, 85, 86, 87, 88, 89

M

Mathematics, 72, 122
Memorable, 37, 41
metaphors, 30
Mexico City, 118
MIT, 8, 36, 104, 105, 113, 114, 122
Mount Holyoke, 110
Music, 27

N

New York, 59, 62

O

Olympics, 118
Omnivore's Dilemma, 39
Opening Hook, 35, 53
Oxford, 15

P

parents, 15, 40, 41, 57, 60, 76, 78, 90, 91, 92, 94, 101, 109
Physics, 70, 72
President, 15, 17, 24, 32, 70, 81, 85
Princeton, 8, 122
Prompts, 20
Psychology, 70, 72, 83, 87

R

rankings, 116
Reality, 117
recommendations, 12, 111
research, 21, 28, 70, 73, 84, 87, 107, 108
Reviewers, 24
Revision, 42
Roommate, 100
Russian Literature, 108

S

SAT, 12, 13, 90
scholarships, 8
Self-motivated, 15, 118, 119
self-motivation, 13, 14, 15, 30, 118
serpentine, 44
seven step program, 10
Seven-Step, 18
Shakespeare, 41
Silicon Valley, 9, 122
Social Contract, 64, 67
South Asian, 60
Stanford, 8, 36, 101, 107, 114, 122

story arc, 10, 18, 26, 30, 77
Stress-free, 114
Stylistic Sins, 42
Supplemental Essays, 106

T

The Hook, 18, 31, 34, 35
Theme Hook, 35, 37, 38
Theorem, 116
Tone deaf, 42, 45
Tufts, 38, 107
Turbulence, 104

U

U. of Chicago, 38, 107
UCs, 38
Unboring, 43
University for California, 80
University of California, 21, 22, 94
University of Pennsylvania, 17

University of Wisconsin Madison, 108, 109
US News & World Report, 115

V

vocabulary, 44, 95
volunteer work, 31, 61

W

Washington DC, 28
Wordlists, 90
Wordy, 42
work experience, 12, 13, 27, 29, 43, 62, 69, 72, 83, 84, 87, 107, 111

Y

Yale, 8, 38, 107, 122
YOLO, 38, 107

Made in the USA
Las Vegas, NV
19 June 2023